the | Names of God

A Devotional Study into What God Says *About Himself*

by

Ellis André

study | guide

Foreword

I had the privilege of being a colleague of Rev. Dr Ellis F. André when we were both on staff at White Rock Baptist Church in the Vancouver area of British Columbia, Canada.

A brilliant yet humble man, he poured his wisdom, knowledge of and relationship with God into every weekly sermon. He was a man gifted by God, given a brilliant brain and communication skills that meant he could help us understand more about God and strengthen our relationship with Him.

It is a blessing that Dr André's family is publishing this study. While he is now experiencing all the fullness of the qualities of God, we are given insight into God's character through the writing of a man who knew Him well.

In this study guide Dr André shows the importance of the different names of God found in scripture, and how each name tells us more about God's character. While designed for small group study, it can be used for an individual's use as well.

The format of the studies is simple and effective, concluding each chapter with a 'nutshell' summary that helps participants focus on what they should remember.

Dr André has left us an excellent tool to enhance our understanding of the greatness of God.

Rev. Fay Puddicombe, MA(Leadership) Trinity Western University

table | of Contents

An Introduction: How to Use this Guide   1

Session 1: What's In a Name? | *Yahweh Elohim*   5

Session 2: God's "Proper" Name | *Yahweh*   17

Session 3: Gracious Lord and Master | *Adonai*   25

Session 4: God Most High | *El Elyon*   33

Session 5: The God Who Sees Me | *El Ro'i*   41

Session 6: The All Sufficient God | *El Shaddai*   51

Session 7: The Everlasting God | *El Olam*   61

Session 8: The LORD Will Provide | *Yahweh Yireh*   71

Session 9: The LORD My Banner | *Yahweh Nissi*   81

Session 10: The LORD Who Heals You | *Yahweh Rophecha*   91

Session 11: The LORD is Peace | *Yahweh Shalom*   103

Session 12: The LORD Almighty | *Yahweh Tsavaoth*   117

Session 13: The LORD, My Shepherd | *Yahweh Rō'i*   127

Session 14: The LORD Our Righteousness | *Yahweh Tsidqenu*   137

Session 15: The LORD Who Sanctifies | *Yahweh Meqaddishchem* 147

Session 16: The LORD is There | *Yahweh Shammah*   159

THE NAMES OF GOD

Introduction

How to Use this Study Guide

Welcome to a study that promises to be both enlightening and
enriching. From the outset, we need to establish a general approach.
Obviously each Life Group is unique and will adapt the study to its
own situation and needs, so I am certainly not being prescriptive
about the exact procedure to be followed.

For each study I shall provide:

1.   One or more key scripture passages and some related
      references,
2.   Some questions to help in our understanding of the passages,
3.   An explanation of the meaning of the particular name of God
      covered in the study,
4.   An indication of the name's relevance for our lives,
5.   A brief summary, and
6.   A suggestion as to how awareness of the particular name can
      help us when we pray.

The Goal: Inductive Bible Study
The key factor is the order in which we will do these things. In an
inductive study, we rely heavily on the interaction of the reverent
reader(s) with the passage itself. *Before* you consider my comments
or explanations, you should read the passage and prayerfully consider
what it means. What do you glean *from the passage(s)*? Also, before

you ask, "What does this mean for me, today?" you should ask, "What did it mean for the original readers?" This may seem like the long way round but it is the best way to ascertain what Scripture actually says.

In a Life Group context we also read the passage with our fellow-believers. This helps us to avoid overly-subjective or idiosyncratic interpretations. Sure, when we come to the passage we already have some ideas in mind whether we like it or not, but by seeking to hear *what the passage says* and listening to the other members of the group, we are able to confirm, modify or even correct these ideas. You will notice that I refer to a number of scripture passages. While each of them sheds some light on the subject, it is not imperative that every single passage be read. Reading each one would certainly do us no harm but this may make the study too protracted. **The must-read passages are in bold type**.

In the first study we are attempting to lay a foundation, so the procedure will be a little different. After this we shall be examining at least one passage of Scripture each week in which one of the names of God is revealed or highlighted. Our purpose here is primarily devotional. In his book, *Knowing God*, J. I. Packer states that "a little knowledge *of* God is worth more than a great deal of knowledge *about* him." [1] As we discover truth about God, we can and should integrate this knowledge into our Christian walk and especially into our devotions. We shall certainly learn more about God; more importantly we can come to know and experience him better.

The Names
Here is a list of the names we shall be considering. In the first column the name is in our script. In the second column the name is in the Hebrew script for the benefit of any who can read Hebrew. In the

third column, I have given a simple phonetic guide to pronunciation; the upper case letters indicate which syllable is accented. Although the transcription is far from perfect, it probably serves our purposes better than a more complicated transcription system. In the fourth column I have indicated the most commonly accepted meaning of each name. Being able to pronounce the names exactly is not the most important thing, but it does help us to be able to articulate the words rather than hesitating and saying . . . "that word."

Name	Hebrew	Pronunciation	Meaning
Elohim	אֱלֹהִים	El-o-HEEM	God
Yahweh	יְהֹוָה	Yah-WEH	LORD (Personal Name)
Adonai	אֲדֹנָי	Ah-doe-NAI	Lord (Master)
El Elyon	אֵל עֶלְיוֹן	El El-YOHN	God Most High
El Ro'i	אֵל רֳאִי	El Raw-EE	The God Who Sees Me
El Shaddai	אֵל שַׁדַּי	El Shad-DIE	The All-Sufficient God
El Olam	אֵל עוֹלָם	El Oh-LAM	The Everlasting God
Yahweh Yireh	יְהֹוָה יִרְאֶה	Yah-WEH Yi-REH	The LORD shall Provide
Yahweh Nissi	יְהֹוָה נִסִּי	Yah-WEH Nis-SEE	The LORD our Banner

Yahweh Rophē	יְהוָה רֹפְאֶךָ	Yah-WEH Raw-phē-CHA	The LORD Who Heals You
Yahweh Shalom	יְהוָה שָׁלוֹם	Yah-WEH Sha-LAWM	The LORD is Peace
Yahweh Tsava'ōth	יְהוָה צְבָאוֹת	Yah-WEH Tsa-va-AWTH	The LORD Almighty
Yahweh Rō'i	יְהוָה רֹעִי	Yah-WEH Raw'EE	The LORD My Shepherd
Yahweh Tsidqenu	יְהוָה צִדְקֵנוּ	Yah-WEH Tsid-ke-NOO	The LORD our Righteousness
Yahweh Meqaddesh	יְהוָה מְקַדֵּשׁ	Yah-WEH Me-Kad-DĒSH	The LORD Who Sanctifies
Yahweh Shammah	יְהוָה שָׁמָּה	Yah-WEH Sham-MAH	The LORD is There

So we are ready to go! We will be blessed as we travel through the passages in which these names are introduced. These are Old Testament (Hebrew) names, but they find their ultimate fulfillment in Jesus. That shouldn't surprise us in the least. Remember "no one has ever seen God, but the one and only Son, who is himself God and is in closest relationship with the Father, he has made him known [*exēgēsato*—"exegeted" him] (John 1:18). If Jesus is "the radiance of God's glory and the exact representation of his being" (Heb 1:3), a study of the names of God is bound to lead us to him. We will bow in awe and worship at the magnificence and perfection of God's plan of salvation centered in the Lord Jesus Christ.

A Note to Study Leaders

You will notice that Study 1 takes a different form from the other fifteen studies. That is because it is necessary to lay a foundation. It is also considerably longer and probably requires at least two sessions. In subsequent studies members of the life group should first consider the passage itself before reading the comment. In the first study, it may help to actually read the notes together. Encountering unfamiliar concepts and terms can be intimidating and calls for some application. But the effort is well worth it.

NOTE

[1] J. I. Packer, *Knowing God* (London: Hodder and Stoughton, 1975), 22 (emphasis added).

יְהוָה אֱלֹהִים
Yahweh Elohim

1

What's in a Name?

This study is foundational. For that reason *it takes a different form from subsequent studies.* In this study there is a fair amount of reading to do to orient ourselves to the subject so it may be necessary to spread it over two weeks. Once we have identified the main Hebrew designations for God, it is possible to see the significance of the names (and compound names) from the passages we will study. But first let's put the large stones in place.

Passages: Gen 1:1-5; 2:4-7; Exod 3:13-15; Isa 6:1-8.

Have you ever noticed how many times our attention is drawn to the meaning of names in the Bible?   Changes of name are particularly significant. How would you like to have been named *Maher-shalal-hash-baz*--"Quick to the plunder swift to the spoil" (Isaiah 8:1-4)? Why do you think God sometimes changed a person's name (Gen 17:3-5, 15-17; 25:24-26; 32:28; Matt 16:16-18)? There's more to this subject than we may have imagined, but does it really matter to us in the 21st century?

Was Shakespeare Right?

When we ask, "What's in a name?" we are implying that the words we use to describe people are not, in themselves, that important. In one sense, we are right. The adage itself comes from one of Shakespeare's plays. It was Juliet, who said to Romeo:

What's in a name?
That which we call a rose
by any other name
would smell as sweet.

We tend to regard names as labels, sounds associated with people, rather than as single-word descriptions of the person, summing up their character. But an adage such as this could never have arisen in Israel. To the Israelites names were of real consequence. They virtually represented the person to whom they belonged. A name conveyed something that was distinctive about its bearer. A person was virtually indistinguishable from their name. Many statements in Scripture only make sense when we understand that there was a definite relationship between a name and its bearer (Psalm 7:17; 113:1-3; Prov 18:12; Ezra 6:12; Acts 4:12).

By way of orientation, think for a moment about your own name.

Have you any idea what *your* name means or why you were given that particular name?

Have you ever had a nickname? How did you acquire it?

Names Are a Big Deal in Scripture

Briefly consider the following passages: **Gen 17:3-5**, 15-16; 35:16- 18;
1 Sam 25:25; **Matt 1:21; 16:16-18.**

First, respond to a question about these verses.

What observations can we make from these verses about the
importance God attaches to names?

Now suppose that God had some specific things to say to us about
himself. And suppose that he actually revealed himself to us by
giving us a series of related but distinct names and compound names.
Suppose further that he unfolded these names at defining moments
in his interaction with his people and that they represent important
insights into his character. Suppose that it is really not difficult for us
English-speakers to identify these names and that they enlarge our
vision of God. Suppose also that an awareness of these names and
their meanings can be a great help to us in our walk with the Lord
and particularly in our prayer lives. Wouldn't you think it worthwhile
to consider them?

Two Foundational Names

There is, of course, only one God. When the Bible refers to him, the
two main designations are "God" (over 2550 times in the Old
Testament) and "the LORD" (6828 times). These designations: God
(**Elohim)** and LORD (**Yahweh**) are foundational. Sometimes (as in

Genesis 2:4) these two words are used together (*Yahweh Elohim*—LORD God). In addition, other words are, on occasion, coupled with these designations to highlight important aspects of God's character. When this happens, the essential truth contained in the "foundational" names (*Elohim* or *Yahweh*) is, of course, retained. The additional word does not add to God's character (how could one possibly do that?) but it draws attention to something that the indescribably great God is or does in relation to his people. So, for example, when we speak of *Yahweh Yireh* (or "Jehovah Jireh" –The LORD will provide), the concept of provision is coupled with *all* that is contained in the name *Yahweh.* In this way a particular aspect of God's goodness is highlighted. The meaning is especially rich when we examine the circumstances in which God the name was revealed.

It is therefore important that we lay a solid foundation before we examine the passages in which we are introduced to the compound names of God. Although this introductory study may seem a little theoretical, it is imperative. Once we have established the foundation, we shall be thrilled to see how these names are used in the biblical narratives. Before we go any further, here is some encouraging news.

This is not Rocket Science and You Don't have to be a Hebraist

You can easily learn to identify the names used to describe God in your English Bible. Just follow these guidelines. The translators of the New International Version adopted the practice used in many English translations by rendering the word **Elohim**—God (e.g. **Gen 1:1**), the word **Yahweh**—LORD (all four letters in the upper case), and the word **Adonai**—Lord (capital 'L'; 'ord' in the lower case, e.g. **Psalm 8:1**). Where we read of "the LORD God," it is a rendering of *Yahweh Elohim*. And where we read of "the Sovereign LORD," it is a rendering of *Adonai Yahweh* (e.g. Gen 15:2, 8; 2 Sam 7:18-29). The following chart indicates the way in which the New International Version translates the three main terms used to refer to God and the two combinations of these names.

Names and Combined Names of God
in the New International Version

HEBREW	TRANSLITERATION	NIV TRANSLATION
יְהוָה	Yahweh	LORD
אֱלֹהִים	Elohim	God
אֲדֹנָי	Adonai	Lord
יְהוָה אֱלֹהִים	Yahweh Elohim	LORD God
אֲדֹנָי יְהוָה	Adonai Yahweh	Sovereign LORD

You will also encounter mention of names such as God Almighty (*El Shaddai*) and the LORD Almighty (*Yahweh Tsava'ōth*). Usually, when the compound name first occurs there is a marginal reference identifying the Hebrew term that is being translated. As we progress and we encounter each of these compound names, you will be thrilled and blessed. But we have done enough for now. So let's make sure we have the basics right.

Questions

1.   When you encounter the word "God" in Genesis 1, which word does it 'translate'?

2.   How would you identify the name *"Yahweh"* in your NIV?

3.   The title "Lord" is a translation of which Hebrew word?

4.   How is the composite name *Yahweh Elohim* rendered
_____ in Genesis 2:4 ff.?

5.   Why do you think that the first time we encounter the name *Yahweh* it is used in combination with *Elohim*?

6.   When the title *Adonai* is used with the name *Yahweh (Adonai Yahweh)*, how is the compound term translated?

7. Why do you think David repeatedly uses this compound term as he responds in prayer to God's word to him (2 Sam 7:18-29)?

A Little More Detail

Before we begin to see the spiritual relevance of the names we have encountered so far, a little more detail is in order.

God—*Elohim*
We are introduced to the first 'name' of God in the very first verse of the Bible: "In the beginning **God** created the heavens and the earth." The word is used thirty-two times in chapter 1 alone.

As indicated above, the word translated "God" is **Elohim.** There are four foundational truths that we should note about this name:

1. Although we may see it as a generic term for deity, *Elohim* is used very much as a personal name (e.g. Psalm 63:1). This should not surprise us since there is only one true God.

2. The word *Elohim* is believed to be derived from a Hebrew root meaning "strength" or "might." The main idea conveyed by the name is that of absolute power. "It is agreed among almost all scholars," says R. B. Girdlestone, "that the name *Elohim* signifies the putter forth of power. He is the Being to whom all power belongs."[1] It is God who calls the universe into being by the power of his word. Absolutely everything has its origin in him and he is sovereign over all that exists.

3.   *Elohim* is a plural word but it is used with singular verbs (the suffix "im" is much like our "s" in English). So Genesis 1:1 reads literally: "In the beginning Gods he created the heavens and the earth." It is a mistake (an anachronism) to liken this to the so-called "royal we"—the plural of majesty. Some have suggested that this unusual usage draws attention to the inexhaustible fullness in God. It certainly does. Others have inferred that this plural anticipates the doctrine of the Trinity. While it would be wrong to assert that the first verse in the Bible actually *teaches* that God is triune, the word certainly *allows* for the richness subsequently revealed as God unfolds his trinitarian nature. In fact, these two ideas are complementary: the richness of God's trinitarian life is an important dimension of God's fullness.

4.   Sometimes we encounter a simplified form of *Elohim*, **El**, especially in conjunction with other words (e.g. *El Elyon* and *El Shaddai*; God Most High and God Almighty respectively; Gen 14:18- 24; 35:11-13). *El* was a generic Semitic word for "god" and is used of a Canaanite deity. But where God is referred to as *El*, there is certainly no confusion of him with the Canaanite high god, *El*! The thought of might contained in the word *Elohim* is also present when the word *El* is used. In his prayer Nehemiah refers to the might of *El*: "Now therefore, our God (Elohim), the great, mighty and awesome God (*El*). . . . (Neh 9:32). We encounter the same thought of might and unfettered ability in Psalm 19:1, "The heavens declare the glory of God (*El*)."

There are also a few references to God as **Eloah** (a singular form of Elohim), mainly in the poetic books (especially Job).[2] Its first use is in Deuteronomy 32:15, "He abandoned the God (*Eloah*) who made him and rejected the Rock, his Saviour."

LORD—*Yahweh*

We shall focus on the name *Yahweh* in our next study, so here I shall confine myself to four preliminary observations:

1.   While the other designations of God are used as names, strictly-speaking *Yahweh* is **the** personal or "proper" name by which God has chosen to make himself known (Exodus 3:13-15; 6:2-5; 34:4-7).

2.   It was not as though *Yahweh* was Israel's God in the same way that the other nations had their national deities. *Yahweh* reveals himself as the *only* God. He chose Israel for a special purpose but he is sovereign over all peoples and all things (Isa 40:25-26; 43:10-13).

3.   You may wonder why we are using the name *Yahweh* and not *Jehovah*. There were no written vowels in Hebrew. Vowel points (the dots and dashes we see under Hebrew letters) were introduced when Hebrew was no longer a (widely) spoken language. God's name is represented by four consonants, transliterated YHWH, but the Jews felt it was too holy to pronounce. When they read aloud they substituted the word *Adonai* (Lord). Centuries later, when vowel points were introduced into the consonantal text, the vowels of the word *Adonai* were inserted into the Tetragrammaton (YHWH; JHVH in German). This gives us "Jahovah" (and subsequently *Jehovah*). So, Jehovah would not have been the way the name was originally pronounced. It would be like substituting the vowels of prime minister for those of Stephen Harper, giving us "Stiphen Hirpire." It is widely agreed among Hebrew scholar that *Yahweh* is the most likely pronunciation. It doesn't matter all that much; it is not the vocalization of the name that is important but its meaning.

4.   A contraction of *Yahweh*, **Yah**, is sometimes used, especially in the Psalms. Like the name *Yahweh* it is transliterated LORD. It seems

to be used where the tone is one of celebration and it carries the full significance of *Yahweh* (e. g. Exod 15:2; Psa 68:4; Isa 12:2; 26:4). Many names and some words incorporate the name *Yah* (e. g. *Eliyah* or *Eliyahu* [Elijah] meaning "My God is *Yahweh*"; *halleluyah* [hallelujah], meaning "Praise *Yahweh*.")

Lord—*Adonai*
The word *Adonai* can be used as a general designation for a superior. It is used, for example, to describe the relationship between a slave and his master. In Modern Hebrew, "*Adoni*" is used to mean "Sir." "*Adon*" can even mean Mr.

Significantly, when the word is first used of God in Scripture, it is used in conjunction with *Yahweh*. Abram says, "O *Adonai Yahweh*. . ." (Gen 15:2, 8), much as *Yahweh* was first used in conjunction with *Elohim* (Gen 2:4). Even at this early stage we can say that *Elohim* speaks primarily of God's might and his majesty, *Yahweh*, God's "personal name," speaks of his self-existence and faithfulness, and *Adonai* portrays him as rightful Lord over all creation. Putting this together, we are like bond-slaves of a generous and kind Master.

Deeper Insight into Well-known Passages
It's interesting how an understanding of these names of God gives us deeper insight into the significance of well-known passages. Take Isaiah 6:1-8 for example. The death of King Uzziah must have had quite an influence on young Isaiah (2 Chron 26:15-23). And then the real King appears to him.

o   See if you can identify the names of God used in this passage (Isa 6:1-8). We shall encounter the name "The LORD Almighty" (*Yahweh Tsava'ōth*) later. It is the name David used when confronting Goliath and it was a favourite of the prophets, especially Haggai (1 Sam 17:45-47; Haggai 2:6-9; Zech 4:6).

Putting it All Together

The one God is *Elohim*, he is *Yahweh*, and he is *Adonai*. Our response to him as *Elohim*, the all-powerful God, is wonder and awe. Our response to him as *Yahweh*, the gracious God of the covenant, is love and gratitude. Our response to him as *Adonai*, the Sovereign Lord and Master, is submission and service.

How This Can Help You

o   Have you received some distressing news lately? How can the knowledge that God is indeed *Elohim (all-powerful)*, coupled with the reality that he is *Yahweh*, the ever-faithful One, and *Adonai,* the Sovereign Lord, help you to face the situation?

o   What if our church undertakes a project that is way beyond our natural capacity, but we believe we are being led by the Holy Spirit to undertake this ministry? How does a knowledge of these names help us?

o   If the rays of this revelation converge in Jesus, can you think of New Testament passages in which we see God's qualities and our appropriate response (e. g. 1 Pet 1:18-19)?

In A Nutshell

Summary

Names were important in ancient Israel. God reveals himself to us by giving us a personal name, *Yahweh* (which we will examine in the next study). In addition the word God (*Elohim*) is used as a personal name. The word *Adonai* means Lord or Master and denotes sovereignty or lordship.

It is possible for readers of the English Bible to know when the words *Yahweh, Elohim* and *Adonai* are used. *Yahweh* is rendered LORD (upper case letters), *Elohim* is rendered God, and *Adonai* is rendered Lord. When the name *Yahweh* is used in conjunction with *Elohim*, the compound term is rendered "the LORD God." When the name *Yahweh* is used in conjunction with *Adonai*, the compound term is rendered "Sovereign LORD."

In addition, a shortened form of *Elohim* (*El*) is combined with other words to form compound titles (e.g. *El Shaddai*). Similarly, words are sometimes suffixed to *Yahweh* to give us compound titles (e.g. *Yahweh Yireh*).

The one God is *Elohim*, he is *Yahweh*, and he is *Adonai*. Our response to him as *Elohim*, the all-powerful God, is wonder and awe. Our response to him as *Yahweh*, the gracious God of the covenant, is love and gratitude. Our response to him as *Adonai*, the Sovereign Lord and Master, is submission and service.

A Prayer

Elohim, Mighty One, you made everything out of nothing, imposed order on chaos, gave birth to beauty, and called it all good. Help me to know you as the one true God who created everything and everyone, the one who has placed me on earth for a purpose—to magnify your name.[3]

Yahweh, compassionate and gracious LORD, you sought us when we were not seeking you. You demonstrated your love for us while we were still sinners. And you are faithful even when we are faithless. We rest in your love.

Adonai, our Sovereign Lord and Master, thank you for the honor of serving you. I know that I was bought at a price and I am not my own. I am so glad I belong to you. Please give me the grace to live in obedience to your will. Amen.

NOTES

[1] R. B. Girdlestone cited in Herbert F. Stevenson, *Titles of the Triune God: Studies in Divine Self-Revelation* (London: Marshall, Morgan and Scott, 1955), 16.

[2] Scholars differ on whether *Elohim* should be regarded as the plural form of *El* (or of *Eloah* for that matter).

[3] Ann Spangler, *Praying the Names of God* (Grand Rapids, MI: Zondervan, 2004), 17.

יְהוָה
Yahweh

2

God's 'Proper' Name

As we encounter the compound names of God in Scripture, we notice that they are sometimes associated with specific incidents, places, altars, or memorials. God reveals himself not so much in a series of theoretical propositions but in dynamic interaction with his people. Before we proceed to examine each of these names, we need to look a little more closely at the name *Yahweh*.

Reminder

Please read the passages first, then consider the questions, and *only then* read the comment. It is not necessary to read the comment in the Life Group (although some may wish to refer to the comment as part of the group discussion). The important thing is that you interact with scripture itself and derive your insights from your reflection on the scripture passages.

Passages and References

Passages   Exod 3:13-15; 6:1-8; 34:4-7.

References
Gen 4:26; 15:7; Psalm 11:7; **Isa 42:8; 43:10-13**; Jer 31:3.

Questions

1. The three passages from Exodus help to convey the essential meaning of the name *Yahweh*. It is associated with God's declaration, "I AM WHO I AM." (*Yahweh* with *Ehyeh asher Ehyeh*). What, if anything, does this tell us about God?

2. From the context in which God reveals himself as *Yahweh*, which three of these terms do you think **most** appropriately convey the meaning of this name?

Powerful	Awesome	Holy	Covenant Partner
Self-existent	Just	Loving	Relational
Merciful	Redeemer	Transcendent	Gracious

Makes one think, doesn't it? Explain to the group what in the passages influenced your choice.

3. Why do you think Moses asked God to reveal his name?

4. What do these passages reveal about what was (and is) in God's heart for his people?

5. In terms of your own salvation, what does the name *Yahweh* mean to you?

6. In what way(s) can an awareness of the meaning of the name *Yahweh* help you when you pray?

Comment

How do we ascertain the meaning of a name? There are three main criteria: (1) we ask if there are etymological (word origin) clues, (2) we pay careful attention to the usage of the name throughout Scripture, and (3) we consider the particular circumstances in which it is introduced (e.g. *Yahweh Yireh* in Genesis 22). We now turn to the meaning of God's personal name, **Yahweh**.

We are exactly not sure when and how God first revealed himself as *Yahweh* (see Gen 4:1, 26; 15:2, 7).[1] But very early in human history, people began to call on the name of *Yahweh* (Gen 4:26). We hear

God say to Abram, "I am *Yahweh* who brought you out of Ur of the Chaldeans to give you this land to take possession of it" (Gen 15:7).

What is most important is the way God explains the meaning of his name to his people. One day Moses saw an acacia bush on fire in the distance. To his amazement he noticed that this particular bush just kept on burning. As he approached it, God called him from within the bush: "Take off your sandals for the place where you are standing is holy ground" (Exod 3:5). He announced to Moses that he was going to deliver his people from Egyptian bondage. Moses, as we know, raised several objections. In the course of the dialogue, God identified himself by name.

In all likelihood, the name *Yahweh* is derived from the same root as the word for "I am" (*ehyeh*). The Old Testament scholar, Th. C. Vriezen, expresses part of the intent of "I AM WHO I AM" rather well: "I myself am there; count on me."[2] David Pawson makes the same point in a more prosaic way when he says, "[The] very name, 'Yahweh', is a participle of the Hebrew verb 'to be'. The English word which conveys the nature of God contained in the name 'Yahweh' is 'always': he has *always* been who he is and will *always* be just the same."[3] Kenneth Hemphill also draws attention to the origin of the name in the imperfect stem of the Hebrew verb 'to be' and points out that "the imperfect tense denotes an action that started in the past, continues in the present, but is not yet complete" and suggests the paraphrase, "I am who I have always been."[4]

It is important that we don't regard God's self-existence and eternality merely as theoretical assertions regarding his attributes. We are saying far more than that he is uncreated and that he lives forever. He is the source of his own life and of all created life. The fact that he is, has always been, and will always be means that he is one hundred percent reliable (Isa 40:28-31). To put it differently, we need to think of the eternality of the living God in *qualitative* rather than *quantitative* terms.

The thought of God's self-existence conveyed by the name *Yahweh* is graphically portrayed by the burning bush that was not consumed. Contrary to nature, it did not derive its "life" from the surrounding environment. The "life" of Yahweh is independent and self-sustaining. Every creature derives its life from another. But he is the source of his own life. In the Revelation he is described as the One "who is and who was and who is to come" (Rev 1:8).

But there is more to this than God's self-sufficiency and his eternality. He is always the same, not as a dull, static being, imprisoned within his own immutability, but as the living God, whose every action is consistent with his perfect nature. For this very reason he is faithful. The redemption which he has brought us testifies to the rich and dynamic nature of his constancy. Think of it: he is present and he is faithful. He is the One who says, "I am always there; you can count on me."

And there is still more. If the etymology of the name lays emphasis on God's self-existence, the context in which the name is explained draws our attention to God's faithfulness as the Saviour of his people. As God prepared Moses to lead the people out of Egypt, he explained, "*I am Yahweh.* I appeared to Abram, Isaac and Jacob as God Almighty (*El Shaddai*), but by my name *Yahweh* I did not make myself known to them. I also established my covenant with them. . . . (Exod 6:2-4). Although this was not the first mention of the name *Yahweh*, it involved a particular explanation of the meaning of the name befitting the new chapter in God's dealings with his people. The LORD explains to the Israelites:

I am *Yahweh* and I will bring you out from under the yoke of the Egyptians. I will free you from being slaves to them, and will redeem you with an outstretched arm and with mighty acts of judgment. I will take you as my own people, and I will be your God. Then you will know that I am *Yahweh,* your God who brought you out from under the yoke of the Egyptians. And I will bring you to the land I swore with uplifted hand to give to Abraham and to Isaac and to Jacob. I will give it to you as a possession. *I am Yahweh* (Exod 6:6-8).

Probably the closest we come to a biblical "definition" of the name Yahweh (although no definition could ever do him justice) is found in Exodus 34:

Then *Yahweh* came down in the cloud and stood there with [Moses] and proclaimed his name Yahweh. And he passed in front of Moses proclaiming, "*Yahweh, Yahweh*, the compassionate and gracious God, slow to anger, abounding in love and faithfulness, maintaining love to thousands, and forgiving wickedness, rebellion and sin. Yet he does not leave the guilty unpunished; he punishes their children and their children's children for the sin of their fathers to the third and the fourth generation (Exod 34:5-7).

We obtain a fuller picture of God's nature as revelation unfolds, but his very name reveals him as the Eternal One, gracious and holy, self-sustaining and ever-present. Nathan Stone identifies the main attributes contained in the name: "God's personal existence, the continuity of his dealings with man, the unchangeableness of his promises, and the whole revelation of his redeeming mercy gathers round the name *Jehovah* [*Yahweh*]."[5] It is in the nature of *Yahweh* to be faithful. He is the God who created us so that we could enjoy a relationship with him. He is the covenant-keeping God. He has gone to incredible lengths to restore us to that relationship. It is not by accident that Joseph was instructed to call his stepson Jesus (*Yeshua* is a contraction of *Yehoshua*, "*Yahweh* is salvation"). *Yahweh* is certainly all-powerful but the focus is not on his might, as such; it is on the *relationship* he has with his people.

In A Nutshell

A Summary
We do not know exactly when God first revealed his name *Yahweh*, but we know that he explained the meaning of the name to Moses (Exodus 3:13-15; 6:1-8; 34:4-7). The name is associated with the Hebrew verb "to be". "I AM WHO I AM" is not an abstract statement about existence but refers to God as the one who is actively present ('I myself am there; you can count on me"). *Yahweh* is the faithful God who establishes his covenant and goes to incredible lengths to show grace to his unfaithful covenant partner. Nowhere is his nature as Yahweh better revealed than when, at great cost to himself, he gave his Son to reconcile us to himself (Rom 5:6-11).

A Prayer

(This prayer is based on David's prayer in 2 Sam 7:18-29 in which David repeatedly addresses God as "Sovereign LORD" [*Adonai Yahweh*]. God had promised to establish David's house forever and David responds in prayer. This promise is ultimately fulfilled in Jesus.

As David marveled at God's gracious promise, we may respond in gratitude for God's amazing grace to us in Jesus.

Lord *Yahweh*, who am I that you have brought me thus far? You have drawn me to yourself and given me "great and precious promises." More than that, you have given me "an inheritance that can never perish, spoil or fade."
What can I say, Lord *Yahweh*? You know me and you have revealed your will to me.

How great you are, Lord *Yahweh*. There is no-one like you and there is no God but you. You have called us to yourself. "Once we were not a people but now we are the people of God; once we had not received mercy but now we have received mercy." We did not deserve your grace but you have made us your own people. You have called us to be "the light of the world," to "declare the praises of him who called us out of darkness into your wonderful light."

Now *Yahweh*, our God (*Yahweh Elohim*), fulfill your word so that your name will be honored forever and people will say, "*Yahweh*, the Almighty (*Yahweh Tsava'ōth*) is God over his people."

O *Yahweh* Almighty, I have boldness to pray in this way because you have revealed your goodness to me. Lord *Yahweh*, you are God. Your words are trustworthy, and you have promised good things to your servant. Please bless me, Lord *Yahweh*, so that your great name will be glorified through my life.

Amen.

NOTES

[1] It is possible to interpret Exodus 3 and 6 as meaning that God announced his name *Yahweh* for the very first time to Moses. Those who interpret the passage this way usually see the earlier references to the name *Yahweh* as anachronistic. In other words, looking back after God's revelation to Moses (when the Torah [Gen-Deut] was written) it was natural to refer to God as LORD (*Yahweh*), whether or not he was actually known by that name when the pre-Exodus incidents occurred. All things considered, it is probably best to understand the Exodus passages as a revelation of the full significance of the name rather than the introduction of a new name for the very first time.

[2] Th. C. Vriezen, *An Outline of Old Testament Theology,* 2nd ed. (Wageningen, The Netherlands: H. Veenman and Zonen nv, 1970), 180. The Hebrew verb "to be" does not convey the abstract notion of being implied in the Greek and modern contexts. "On the contrary, God is in Israel the One who is always really present" (Ibid.,181).

[3] J. David Pawson, *Unlocking the Bible* (London: HarperCollins, 2003), 28, 100-101, emphasis added.

[4] Kenneth Hemphill, *The Names of God* (Nashville, TN: Broadman and Holman Publishers, 2001), 70.

[5] Nathan Stone, *Names of God* (Chicago, IL: Moody Publishers, 1944, 2010 ed.), 37.

אֲדֹנָי

Adonai

3

Gracious Lord and Master

There is one more important title we must consider before we proceed to the compound titles that are formed by attaching suffixes to the name *El*. As mentioned briefly in study 1, *Adonai* is a title that lays emphasis on God's sovereignty.

Passage and References

As you read the primary passages and the references, bear in mind that in the NIV the word *Yahweh* is rendered LORD, *Adonai* is rendered Lord, and *Adonai Yahweh*, Sovereign LORD (Lord God in the KJV).

Passages: Judg. 6:11-24; Isa. 6:1-8.
The appearance of the LORD to Gideon may well seem strange to us. Actually this is an amazing account. At this point I need simply to remark that the word *Adoni* is rendered "Sir" in verse 13 and *Adonai* "Lord" in verse 15. I shall also briefly discuss the reference to "The Angel of Yahweh" in the Comment below.

References
    Gen. 15:1-8; Exod. 4:10-13; 2 Sam. 7:18-29; **Ps. 8: 1**; **110:1 (cf. Matt. 22:41-45; Acts 2:34-36)**; Exod. 21:2-11; Dan. 9:4-5; John 13:12-17; Rom. 1:1; 12:1; 1 Cor. 6:18-20; Gal. 6:17; 1 Pet. 1:18-19.

Questions

Our focus is on two passages: Judg. 6:11-24 and Isa. 6:1-8.

1. **JUDGES 6:11-24.** What, in the text, makes us think that Gideon knew that his visitor was an exceptional person?

2. Do you think he realized that this was the Angel of *Yahweh*? Why or why not?

3. When he addresses his visitor as *Adoni* in verse 13, has he caught on to the identity of his visitor?

4. Who do you think the "Angel (messenger) of *Yahweh*" is in this passage? And what leads you to that conclusion?

5. What do you think led Gideon to the conclusion that he was actually meeting with God (a theophany; see below)?

6. Why did Gideon fear for his life?

7. What would your reaction be if God appeared to you in this way? Do you think it is possible? Do you think it is likely? Why/Why not?

8. **ISAIAH 6:1-8.** Do you think that the first seven words of the passage are simply a chronological reference, or is there more to it than that? (2 Chron. 26:15-16, 20-21)

9. Why do you think Isaiah uses the word "Lord" (*Adonai*) to refer the LORD Almighty (*Yahweh Tsava'ōth*) in this passage?

10. Do you see any relationship between the fact that it was *Adonai* who addressed the prophet and the prophet's response? If so, what?

11. Is there some incongruity in the responses of Moses and Peter to one whom they address as Lord in Exod 4:10-14 and Acts 10:14 - 15:29; 11:17 (*Adonai* in Hebrew; *Kurios* in Greek)?

12. Have you ever made the same mistake as Moses and Peter? If so, how best can we avoid doing so in the future?

Comment

The word *Adoni* ("*my lord*") is often used as a term of respect or a general designation for a superior. In modern Hebrew, *Adoni* is used to mean "Sir" and *Adon* can even mean "Mr". Two hundred and fifteen of the nearly 300 times that the word is used in the Old Testament, it refers to men. When it is used of men it is always in the singular (*adon or adoni*) and when it is used of God it is always in the plural (*Adonai*).[1]

The twin concepts conveyed by the word are lordship and ownership. Probably the best way to understand the word is to see it in the light of the relationship between a master and a slave. Nowadays we have an entirely negative picture of the inhuman practice of slavery. What we tend to overlook is the fact that in Bible days a slave was often better off than a hired servant. True, the slave was the possession of his/her master and completely at their disposal. A cruel or abusive *adon* could certainly exploit a hapless slave. But we have to envisage a situation in which there is such love and devotion that a slave voluntarily renounces his right to freedom (Exod 21:2- 11). Such is his confidence in his master, that he is *eager* to continue in submission and obedience.

Nathan Stone observes that "the purchased slave stood in a much nearer relationship to his lord than the hired servant. . . . The slave had the right of his master's protection and help and direction. Nor was the relationship devoid of affection."[2] Instead of focusing on the negative associations of slavery with bondage and exploitation, we have to identify the ideas of benevolent possession and affection.

Adonai Meets with Gideon

It is significant that when the word is first used of God, it is used in conjunction with *Yahweh*: Abram says, "O *Adonai Yahweh* . . ." (Gen 15:2, 8). The first time *Yahweh* was used, it was used in conjunction with *Elohim* (Gen 2:4); here *Adonai* is linked with *Yahweh*. We have already noticed that the name *Elohim* speaks of God's might and his majesty and *Yahweh*, God's "personal name," lays emphasis on his self-existence and faithfulness. The name *Adonai* portrays him as the One who is rightful Lord over all creation. He created everything; he sustains everything; and he is sovereign.

One can see the irony (and audacity) of Moses addressing God as *Adonai* but unwilling to follow his directions (Exod 4:10-17). The account of Gideon's call constitutes the clearest instance of the use of the word *Adonai* in relation to the name *Yahweh* (Judges 6: 11-24). A few elucidatory comments may prove helpful. In this and some other passages where we read of the "angel of the LORD," reference is being made, not to an angel as such, but to an appearance of God in angelic form (Gen 16:7, 13; 22:11-15; Exod 3:2; Num 22:21-35; Judges 2:1-5; 1 Kings 19:3-9; 2 Kings 1:3-4; Zech 3:1-9; 12:8) . In other words, this is a theophany. Some commentators boldly describe such appearances as pre-incarnation appearances of the Son, the second Person of the Trinity. Passages such as this certainly incline us toward such a view.

We notice in this passage that the names *Yahweh, Adonai* and *Elohim* are used interchangeably to describe the mysterious Visitor. At first Gideon was not quite sure of the identity of the Visitor but he was apparently aware that he was more than just some passer-by. So he used a term of respect when addressing him. All the references to *Yahweh* before Gideon's exclamation in verse 22 form part of the narration (the narrator knows it was *Yahweh*; at first, Gideon didn't). When fire flared from the rock and the Visitor disappeared, Gideon exclaimed "Ah *Adonai Yahweh*," fearing he might die, and he built an altar to the one who had said to him, "Peace! Do not be afraid. You are not going to die." The fact that he called the altar *Yahweh Shalom* is a clear indication that he realized the Visitor was *Yahweh*.

Isaiah "Sees" *Adonai*
It is reasonable to infer that the ignominious death of King Uzziah was a disappointment to the young Isaiah (2 Chron 26:15-23). The earthly king who had shown such promise had toppled unceremoniously from his throne. But then Isaiah had a vision of *Adonai* who is worshipped as *Yahweh Tsava'ōth* (Isa 6:1-8). The task assigned to him was an extremely difficult one but he had met the real King, *Adonai*, and obedience was the appropriate response.

Both Gideon and Isaiah were called to obedience and both made a conscious decision to submit to God's authority as a bond slave would submit to the authority of their master. *Adonai* is the Lord whose word is to be heeded. Total obedience is the appropriate response. But the relationship is not one of servile bondage.

Significantly, whenever *Adonai* commissions a person, he provides the wherewithal to accomplish the task. God was grieved that Moses protested that he was not competent for the mission (Exod 4:10-11). Gideon had to know that *Adonai* would give him and his army the necessary strength (Judges 6:15-16). Isaiah's lips were cleansed and he bowed in submission to *Adonai* (Isa 6:5-8). Interestingly the shrinking Jeremiah also adjudged himself incompetent for the task, but addressed God as *Adonai Yahweh* and was obedient to the call (Jer 1: 4-10, 19). Kenneth Hemphill makes the valid observation that "those who acknowledge God as *Adonai* will always exhibit three characteristics: (1) they acknowledge themselves as servants . . , (2) they understand that their Master can supply all their need, and (3) they realize that they can do whatever God calls them to do."[3]

The principle applies in the New Testament where Jesus is called Lord. All that is said of God as *Adonai* applies to him (John 13:13-17; Acts 2:36; 1 Cor 1:2). It is no accident that Paul's favorite self-designation was slave (*doulos*; Rom 1:1). We are all indebted to our Lord. He has a double right to be our Master. He is *Adonai* and he has redeemed us (1 Pet 1:18-19). "Do you not know that your body is a temple of the Holy Spirit who is in you, whom you have received from God? You are not your own. You were bought at a price. Therefore honour God with your body" (1 Cor 6:19-20).

In A Nutshell

A Summary

Adonai means Lord. When the term is used, God is recognized as the one who has both the wisdom and the right to command our total obedience. The image that best depicts the meaning of *Adonai* is that of a benevolent master/slave owner. We have to envisage a situation in which there is such love and devotion that a slave voluntarily renounces their right to emancipation, saying, "I love my Master . . . and do not want to go free" (Exod. 21:2-11). Such is his confidence in his master and the recognition of the appropriateness of the relationship that they are eager to continue in submission and service. For Paul, the designation "slave (*doulos*) of Christ Jesus" was an honour.

The Lord Jesus is our *Adonai,* having purchased us at an inestimably great price (John 13:12-17; 1 Cor. 6:18-20; 1 Pet. 1:18-19). There is no greater honour than to call him Lord (Acts 2:36; Rom. 10:9-10; 1 Cor. 1:2).

A Prayer

It is not surprising that in a prayer of national confession, Daniel repeatedly refers to God as *Adonai* (Dan. 9:4-19).

Sovereign Lord, we bow before you as our gracious Master. You have purchased us at so great a price that we cannot adequately grasp its immensity. We have surrendered to you and we call you Lord from our hearts. We have heeded your call to present our bodies as a living sacrifice, holy and pleasing to you.

But Lord, we have to confess that we so easily withdraw our lives from the altar. Today we re-consecrate ourselves to you. We willingly defer to your wisdom and your goodness. You are Lord! We thank you that we are in perfect hands when we surrender to you. Thank you for the honor of being part of your household. Lord, we know that you never call us to anything without enabling us. Help us to trust you in such a way that we respond to your commands without protest or hesitation.

You are our Lord. We pray that our lives will bear eloquent testimony to that fact. We are honoured to be called your servants. May you be glorified as Lord forever! Amen.

NOTES

[1] *Adonai* is grammatically plural and has a possessive suffix. "It is possible that the plural *Adonai* is used to enhance, or underline and exalt the awesome majesty of God." Kenneth Hemphill, *The Names of God* (Nashville, TN: Broadman and Holman Publishers, 2001), 22.

[2] Nathan Stone, *Names of God* (Chicago, IL: Moody Publishers, 2010), 64.

[3] Hemphill, *The Names of God*, 32-33.

אֵל עֶלְיוֹן
El Elyon
4

God Most High

We come to the first of the compound names of God. The way the name is used in Scripture is highly significant for several reasons. During biblical times, the designation *El* was sometimes used as a general reference to deity in the nations surrounding Israel. It is also true that *El* was the name of one of the gods of the Canaanites. But, as we will see, Scripture reserves the name *El Elyon* for *Yahweh* and attributes transcendence and sovereignty to him. The Bible sometimes refers to God as *El Elyon* (God Most High), but usually it refers to him simply as *Elyon* (The Most High). I should also mention before we engage with the study's four focal passages that Daniel 4 was written in Aramaic[1] where the word used for the Most High in Daniel 4:34-37 is *Illaya,* which is derived from the same root as *Elyon*.

Passages and References

Passages: **Gen. 14:18-24 (cf. Heb. 7:1-3); Isa. 14:12-15; Dan. 4:34- 37; Psa. 91:1, 2, 9, 10** (note the juxtaposition of the divine names).

References

Deut. 32: 3, 4, 8; 2 Sam. 22: 13, 14, 17; Psa. 57:1-3; 83:18; Eccl. 5:1-7; Luke 1:32, 35; 8:28; **Acts 4:23-31;** 7:48-50.

Questions

1. From your reading of the above passages, how would you explain the meaning of *El Elyon* to a new Christian?

2. **GENESIS 14: 18-24; HEBREWS 7:1-3.** Who do you think Melchizedek was?

3. Was he a priest of one of the Canaanite gods or did he serve the same God as Abram?

4. So, would you think there was true religion outside of Israel?

5. What evidence do you find *in the text* that *El Elyon* was indeed *Yahweh*?

6. What attribute(s) of God is (are) highlighted by the name?

7. **ISAIAH 14:12-14.** Irrespective of who the king of Babylon was (see comment below), what does this passage tell us (1) about him, and (2) about God?

8. **DANIEL 4:34-37.** What do you find significant about Nebuchadnezzar's confession?

9. **PSALM 91:1, 2, 7-10.** In what circumstances do you think the realization that God is *El Elyon* is particularly relevant for us?

10. Which of the following words *best* describe the meaning of *El Elyon*? Why do you think so?

Distant	Ever-present	Sovereign	Powerful	Exalted

11. **ACTS 4:23-31.** How ought the realization that God is indeed *El Elyon* to affect our prayer lives?

Comment

Four passages, in particular, help us to gain a biblical perspective on the name *El Elyon*. In addition, the "references" highlight the devotional value of experiencing God as *El Elyon*.

Melchizedek and God Most High (Gen 14:18-24)

One of the most interesting characters in the Bible is a man called Melchizedek. He appears suddenly in the life of Abram and, just as quickly, he disappears and we never hear of him again (except for a cryptic reference in Psa 110 and in Hebrews). An alliance of foreign kings had invaded the cities of Sodom and Gomorrah, taken captives and seized their goods. Abram had pursued them, rescued the captives and retrieved the booty. This made him something of a hero and the king of Sodom came out to meet him upon his return. So did the king of Salem (Jerusalem), who brought out bread and wine. Abram recognised the king of Salem as a priest of God Most High *(El Elyon)*. He blessed Abram in the name of "God Most High, Creator of heaven and earth who [had] delivered Abram's enemy into his hand." Abram, we are told, gave him a tenth of everything (Gen. 14: 18-20).

Melchizedek was the ruler of Salem, one of the important cities in the region. He was a remarkable man. As a priest of God Most High, he blessed Abram. Significantly, Abram saw him as a representative of

Yahweh when he addressed the king of Sodom: "I have raised my hand to the LORD, God Most High *(Yahweh, El Elyon)*, Creator of heaven and earth, and have taken an oath. . . ." (Gen. 14:22).

The Writer to the Hebrews sees Melchizedek's role as an extremely important one. Indeed, the high priesthood of Jesus was patterned on that of Melchizedek (Heb. 5:10; 7:1-28). He notes the significance of the man's name, which means "king of righteousness" and the fact that he was king of Salem (meaning peace). Of consequence for us here is the fact that as a priest of *El Elyon* he was also a priest of *Yahweh*. *El Elyon,* the Creator of heaven and earth, had granted Abram victory, demonstrating that he was ruler over events on earth. This designation is more than an abstract attestation of God's exalted position. It conveys his sovereignty, and his superintendence of the events of history.

The King of Babylon who Aspired to be like the Most High (Isa 14:12-15)
This passage has often been cited as the account of the fall of Satan (Lucifer).[2] It's not difficult to understand why it has been understood to depict Lucifer's expulsion from heaven (as has Ezek.28: 11-19). It is assumed that, just as certain prophecies look forward beyond the immediate events of the day, so this prophecy, addressed to the king of Babylon, also has a wider reference and looks back to Satan's rebellion, whose attitude the king was emulating. This, some commentators argue, is plausible because of the link throughout Scripture between Babylon and satanic rebellion against God (Gen. 11:1-9; Rev. 17-18). There are not sufficient grounds for such an inference, but we do at least have a picture here of the blasphemous extreme to which human arrogance can go, and the consequences of such presumption.

It is important to recognize that the king who was "cast down" aspired to be "like the Most High (*Elyon*)," raising his throne "above the stars of God." When any creature sets itself up against *El Elyon*, there can be only one result: abasement.

Nebuchadnezzar's Acknowledgement

God appointed the Babylonians to be the captors and overlords of his people. Since some of the Jews rose, as they usually do, to high positions, it was inevitable that monarchs would be forced to compare their deities with the unseen God of Israel. As a heathen king of the most powerful empire on earth, Nebuchadnezzar became proud. His humiliation and subsequent recognition of God's sovereignty makes a fascinating reading. On a smaller scale one has seen God humble people, but Nebuchadnezzar's temporary insanity must be one of the most dramatic instances of the adage, "whoever exalts himself will be humbled, and whoever humbles himself will be exalted" (Matt. 23: 12). Upon his reinstatement, Nebuchadnezzar acknowledged Israel's God as the Most High.

Read Daniel 4:34-37. Here we have a clear recognition of God's sovereignty. But it is not just raw power and extreme might that is celebrated. "Everything he does is right and all his ways are just" (Dan. 4:37).

Protection

For Moses and for David, the fact that God is the Most High was much more than a theological affirmation. They found comfort in his sovereignty. Moses remembered that it was the Most High "who shielded (Israel) and cared for him; he guarded him as the apple of his eye, like an eagle that stirs up its nest and hovers over its young, and spreads its wings to catch them and carries them on its pinions" (Deut. 32:8-11). For David, the Most High was a rock, a refuge and a saviour (2 Sam. 22:1-3, 14). The Psalmist's usage of the names of God in Psalm 91 is particularly significant. Here, the accent falls on the mention of *Elyon* in the context of God's care and protection:

> He who dwells in the shelter of the Most High *(Elyon)*
> will rest in the shadow of the Almighty *(Shaddai)*.
> I will say of the LORD *(Yahweh),*
> "He is my refuge and my fortress,
> my God *(Elohim),* in whom I trust."
>
> If you say, "The LORD *(Yahweh)* is my refuge,"
> and make the Most High *(Elyon)* your dwelling,
> no harm will overtake you,
> no disaster will come near your tent (Psa. 91: 1-2, 9-10).

New Testament Reality
God has always been *El Elyon* and was recognized as such when the early church raised their voices to him in prayer (Acts 4:23-31). Moreover, it is important to see the way in which the Lord Jesus is destined to occupy the position that belongs to *El Elyon* and is even now seated on the throne (Acts 2:36; Phil. 2:8-11; Eph. 1:18-23; Col. 1:18-20).

Far Above Us *and* Right Here with Us
Transcendence and immanence: that's the way theologians refer to the wonderful reality that God is so great that he towers above us but so near that he dwells with us. This principle is wonderfully enunciated in Isaiah 57:15:

> For this is what the high and exalted one says—
> He who lives forever, whose name is holy:
> "I live in a high and holy place,

but also with those who are contrite and lowly in spirit,
to revive the spirit of the lowly
and to revive the heart of the contrite."

And so, what does the name *El Elyon* convey to us? He is God Most High. Melchizedek represented him. Abraham knew him. The Psalmist rejoiced that he was King over all the earth. It was the Most High who gave the nations their inheritance when he divided all mankind. Nebuchadnezzar discovered that the Most High rules in the affairs of men. He is great, unimaginably great. He is Sovereign. "His dominion is an eternal dominion. No one can hold back his hand or say to him, 'What have you done?'" Even demons are forced to acknowledge his position. The demon-possessed man from the hills on the north-eastern shore of the Sea of Galilee fell before Jesus and the demon cried out: "What do you want with me, Jesus, Son of the Most High God? I beg you, don't torture me!" (Luke 8:28). He is the One who dwells in a high and holy place but also with him who is contrite and lowly in spirit. And he is the One to whom we can go in time of need (Acts 4:23-31).

We may come boldly into his presence, but we may not strut in presumptuously (Eccl. 5:1-7). We may enjoy intimacy with him but this can never mean familiarity or irreverence. We may not approach the Most High with arrogance, but we may certainly approach him with confidence.

In A Nutshell

Summary
We first come across the compound name *El Elyon* (God Most High) or *Elyon* (the Most High) when we meet a man called Melchizedek who was king of Salem (Peace) and whose name meant "king of righteousness." As priest of *El Elyon* he blessed Abram and received a tithe from him. Abram saw *El Elyon* and *Yahweh* as one and the same person. He is the "creator of heaven and earth." In other passages *Elyon* is seen as sovereign. Nebuchadnezzar and another "king of Babylon" discovered that humility is the only appropriate attitude before his majesty (Isa. 14:4, 12-17). Although he is exalted above his creation, he is intimately involved with it. In this as-yet-unredeemed-age, evil is a reality and God's children can expect to face opposition and suffer setbacks. But "God is still on the throne; the Most High is sovereign over all the kingdoms of the earth" (Dan. 4:17, 25, 32, 34, 35). It is good to be reminded of this, especially when circumstances seem to overwhelm us. David asks the question, "When the foundations are being destroyed, what can the righteous do?" He immediately responds, "*Yahweh* is in his holy temple; *Yahweh* is on his heavenly throne" (Psa. 11:3-4).

A Prayer

El Elyon, **God Most High**, Ruler of heaven and earth, we gladly acknowledge you not only as our King but as Sovereign Lord over everything and everyone. We know that we live in a world that is not yet redeemed and evil abounds. But even now, you are God and we can come to you, recognizing your sovereignty.

We worship you as Creator and Sustainer of all that is. And we know that there is no one on earth who does not answer to you. Help us to remember, particularly in difficult times, that when you open a door, no one can shut it, and when you close a door, no one can open it. Help us to learn, as Abraham did, that "nothing is too hard for the LORD." Enable us, like Joseph, to realize that you have a plan, even when we can't see what it is.

You are the Most High and you have no need to prove it. We marvel at your patience and understand that it is precisely because you are sovereign that you do not need to immediately quell all opposition to your rule. Most of all, we marvel that though you dwell in a high and holy place, you also draw near to us. Thank you, LORD. It baffles our minds but it delights our hearts. We honour your name, God Most High.

Amen

NOTES

[1] Aramaic was the common international language of the near East at the time. It is similar to but different from Hebrew. This can be seen, for example, by comparing the Aramaic words of Jesus from the cross (*"Eloi, Eloi, lema sabachthani"*; Mark 15:34) with the Hebrew words of Psalm 22:1, *"Ēlai, Ēlai, lama azavtani."* Dan.1:1-2:4a and 8:1-12:13 were written in Hebrew and Dan. 2:4b-7:28 are in Aramaic.

[2] *Lucifer* is the Latin translation of the Hebrew *hēlēl,* rendered "Morning Star" or "Shining One" in Isa. 14:12.

אֵל רָאִי

El Ro'i

5

The God Who Sees Me

Most of us have felt, at some time or other, that our situation has eluded God's notice. It is one thing to believe in theory that God is omniscient and another altogether to believe that he actually notices *me*, and cares. Before us is a most encouraging account. It assures us that God does "see" us, not with the cold eye of an unconcerned omniscience but with the compassionate eye of a loving Father.

Passages and References

Passages: **Gen. 16:1-16; 21:14-21.**

References
    Psa. 32:8 (cf. Exod. 3:7-8); Psa. 33:18; **139:7-12**; Mark 5:25-34; 2 Tim. 4:1 (literally, "In the sight of God"; 1 Pet. 3:12)

Questions

1.   Can you imagine how desperate Hagar must have been to flee into the desert to escape the anger and bitterness of Sarai? She was Sarai's slave and Sarai's rejection of her must have seemed like God's rejection. What do you think would have made her predicament feel so unbearable?

2. Can you think of a time when you had virtually come to the end of yourself? If so, were you able to reassure yourself that God was fully aware of your situation and would certainly see you through the trial? If not, what made it so difficult for you to do so?

3. What, in your view, is meant by God's omniscience?

4. Do you think Hagar's problem was that she had an inadequate understanding of the omniscience of God?

If not, what do you think her problem was?

Have you ever been there? If so, when?

What, in the passage, is of encouragement to you?

5. What does this account tell us about God's nature?

6. One of the features of Hebrew poetry was parallelism. In other words, a thought is expressed in one line and then repeated in different words, qualified or expanded in another line. Try writing a piece of "Hebrew poetry." The first line is: "You God see me." Add a second and possibly a third and fourth line. The word "see" conveys a particular thought *in this context*. Think of a synonym to use in your second line.

Comment

An "Indecent Proposal"

It is easy to criticize Abram and Sarai for rationalizing and taking the law into their own hands, and it is easy, with the wisdom of hindsight, to see how ill-considered Sarai's suggestion was. But *we* also so easily try to bring God's promises within the realm of possibility. Imagine, Sarai had a young and apparently loyal servant. The two women almost certainly had a good relationship. Hagar must have seemed as worthy a "surrogate" mother as Sarai could hope to find. So Sarai did a nifty bit of spiritualising. She probably knew that what she was doing was questionable to say the least. But, in addressing Abram she made her proposal sound fairly spiritual: "The LORD has kept me from having children. Go sleep with my maidservant; perhaps I can build a family through her"

(Gen. 16:2). She managed to find a loophole in God's promise. God had told Abram, "A son coming from your own body will be your heir" (Gen. 15:4). He had not actually *said* anything about Sarai's body. In the region from which Abram and Sarai had come, contracts have actually been found which obliged a childless wife to provide her husband with a substitute. So the solution seemed reasonable enough. It was, however, "an indecent proposal" to say the least.

The Consequence
Hagar conceived and then the psychological ramifications kicked in. *She* was, after all, carrying Abram's child, the child which Sarai could not bear him. So she despised Sarai to whom the child would legally belong. We are not sure how she displayed her change of attitude, but Sarai soon detected it. So Sarai made Hagar's life unbearable, so much so that Hagar fled from her.

Probably she planned to return to Egypt but, even if she were strong and fit, she would have been unlikely to survive the journey. Anything seemed better than the taunts of Sarai. So she set out. What compounded Hagar's predicament is that she must have felt very much like a "second class" believer. Abram and Sarai were the spiritual ones. God's hand had been upon them. And here she was, not too important in the scheme of things. She had joined them but no great promises had been made to *her*. Our hearts go out to her. This was her darkest hour to date. However she had contributed to the situation by despising Sarai, she now felt the utter loneliness of the outsider. We can only imagine her sense of rejection and injustice. Eventually she found a spring in the desert and sat down, dejected and forsaken.

The Angel of *Yahweh* finds her.
This is the first reference in the Bible to the Angel of *Yahweh*

(mentioned in Study 3). A few further comments may prove helpful. If we examine the references to him in the Old Testament, there is no doubt that he identifies himself with God. Those who met him believed that they had seen the LORD (e.g. Gen. 22: 11 ff; Ex.3:2 ff; Judg. 6: 11-22; Zech. 3:1-10). In addition there are instances where the *term* is not used but the person referred to carries the authority of God, (e.g. Gen. 32:22-32; Josh. 5:13-15). In fact, this is one of the great anticipations of the doctrine of the Trinity. Here is a divine person; he is identified with God and yet he seems to be distinct from God. It makes one think of John 1: 1, "In the beginning was the Word and the Word was *with* God and the Word *was* God" (italics added). Significantly, we never read of *the* Angel of the Lord in the New Testament. The reason for this is simple: He is seated at the right hand of the Father as the ascended Lord Jesus Christ.

He entered into a conversation with Hagar. Please reread 16:7-12 carefully. Imagine the look on Hagar's face: surprise and relief, combined with gratitude and awe. She gave this name to *Yahweh* who spoke to her: *El Ro'i*—"You are the God who sees me (*El Ro'i*)," for she said, "I have now seen the One who sees me." The well where this all took place was called *Be'ēr Lachai Ro'i*--"Well of the Living One who sees me," and the name stuck. The realisation that God was watching over her must have changed her life. It usually does.

El Ro'i "Sees" and Hears Hagar and Ishmael
There is an important sequel to this account (Gen. 21:14-21). Hagar's troubles were far from over. There must have been an uneasy truce in the home. Possibly the ceasefire had more to do with Hagar's attitude than with Sarai's. Fourteen years went by, then, in one of history's most amazing events, Isaac was born to ninety-year-old Sarah. And God's everlasting covenant would be established with

him and his descendants. Ishmael was not forgotten. He would also be protected and blessed, and his descendants would also become a great nation, but the covenant was to be established with Isaac.

Then all the old resentment resurfaced. Abram's name had been changed to Abraham (father of many), and Sarai's name had been changed to Sarah (Princess) in connection with the fulfillment of God's promise that they would have a son. At the feast held to celebrate Isaac's weaning, Sarah caught sight of Ishmael, who was now a young teenager, ridiculing her Isaac. She insisted that Abraham get rid of Hagar and Ishmael. Abraham was devastated but God confirmed to him that the time had come for Hagar and Ishmael to leave. In what must have been a traumatic experience, Abraham provided Hagar with some provisions and sent her and Ishmael on their way.

They wandered in the desert of Beersheba. Eventually they ran out of water. It's terribly hot in that area. She could not bear to watch her son die so she put him under one of the bushes and sat down some distance away. Ishmael was afraid and, realising that this was probably the end, he began to sob. Once again Hagar had reached the end of herself. My guess is that she was sobbing too. How does a mother feel in such circumstances?

But just as God had seen and heard Hagar fourteen years before, so he heard Ishmael's cry. He spoke to her once again: "What is the matter, Hagar? Do not be afraid; I have heard the boy crying as he lies there. Lift the boy up and take him by the hand, for I will make him into a great nation." God then opened her eyes and she saw a well of water and gave Ishmael something to drink. Once again God had proved that he both sees and hears in times of distress.

Under God's Eye

In fact, it is not by chance that we find references to God's eyes in both testaments. God assured David of his personal interest. I find the idiom particularly interesting:

I will instruct you and teach you in the way you should go; I will counsel you and watch over you." That reads literally: "on you (shall be) my eye." One translation reads: "I will guide you with my eye upon you" (Psa. 32:8).

The same idea is conveyed in Psalm 33:18, "The eyes of the LORD are on those who fear him; on those who hope in his unfailing love."

When we turn to the New Testament, we encounter the same thought: "For the eyes of the Lord are on the righteous and his ears are attentive to their prayer. . . ." (I Pet. 3:12). And when God "sees" us, he is not looking on with the wide-angle lens of omniscience. He *focuses* on us with concern. What do you think he meant when he said to Moses: "I have indeed *seen* the misery of my people in Egypt . . . and I am concerned about their suffering. So I have come down to rescue them from the hand of the Egyptians. . . ."(Exod. 3:7-8; emphasis added)?

There is another dimension to this reassuring truth. It liberates us from the need to try to impress others. Paul makes the valid point to Timothy that we all live "in the presence of God." Literally, the words used in the original (2 Tim. 4:1), mean "in (or under) the sight of God." Paul was saying to his young protégée, "Timothy, all that you do — all that you will ever do — is seen by God and known to him. He never takes his eye off you."

That may seem inhibiting; in fact it is liberating. It sets us free from every other concern. Our Lord was saying the same thing when he warned his disciples to "be careful not to (perform their) acts of righteousness before others, to be seen by them. If you do you will have no reward from your Father in heaven. So when you give to the needy do not announce it with trumpets. . . . Then your Father, who sees what is done in secret, will reward you" (Matt. 6: 1-4).

Too Insignificant?

Let's return, for a moment, to Hagar. She called the well "*Be'ēr Lachai Ro'i*——Well of the Living One who sees me." What a revelation to her. She was only Sarai's servant! She may have thought of her spiritual standing as "by association." Why should God see *her* of all people? And many people feel as unimportant as she did. From a spiritual point of view, they don't really believe they have caught God's attention. They imagine that they may be able to obtain some spiritual benefits anonymously, like the woman who touched the hem of Jesus' garment, but they think they are too unimportant to attract his personal attention (Mark 5:25-34). The "spiritual giants" feature in God's plans, but he does not pay too much attention to them, or so they think.

But the words of Psalm 139 apply to *all* of us who call on the name of the Lord:

Where can I go from your Spirit?
Where can I flee from your presence?
If I go to the heavens, you are there;
If I make my bed in the depths,
you are there.
if I rise on the wings of the dawn,
if I settle on the far side of the sea,
even there your hand will guide me,
your right hand will hold me fast.

If I say, "Surely the darkness will hide me
and the light become night around me,"
even the darkness will not be dark to you;
the night will shine like the day,
for darkness is as light to you
(Psalm 139:7- 12).

We need to remember at all times, but especially at the low points in our lives, that we never pass from God's field of vision. Moreover, for God, to see is to care. When I am at the point of extremity, there is one thing I need to know more than anything else in the world: the God I serve is *El Ro'i*--the God who sees me.

In A Nutshell

Summary
The title *El Ro'i* is used only once in Scripture but its use, in connection with the plight of Hagar, is highly significant. It expresses the important truth that God sees us and this refers to far more than his omniscience. In the case of Hagar and Ishmael, God's eye was certainly upon them. It is easy, in our times of extremity, to feel that we have passed beyond God's vision, or at least beyond his care. Some of us may feel that we may have connected with the spiritual benefits that accrue for everyone but that we remain more or less anonymous. For whatever reason we feel unworthy of God's personal attention (see Mark 5:25-34). Well *El Ro'i* is simply not like that. He is the God who sees me! And "seeing," in this sense, means caring.

A Prayer

Loving Father, I so easily forget that your eye is always upon me. In the barren times I think that your attention is focused elsewhere. What a comfort it is to know that even in the wilderness you see me.

Help me to know, especially in the difficult times, that I am never out of your sight. I know you can see all things and that nothing in creation is hidden from your sight (Heb 4:13). But I do not want to think of that merely as a quality of omniscience.

I have two requests. First, Lord, help me to be open and honest with you. I know that simply accepting that nothing is hidden from you is not enough. Help me to be *willing* to be known by you, so much so, that if I could hide my inmost thoughts from you, I would not want to do so. Then Lord, when for whatever reason I feel forsaken, please remind me that you are *El Ro'i*, that you see me and care for me more than I could ever know.

Thank you for your unfailing love. I know that nothing "is able to separate us from the love of God that is in Christ Jesus our Lord" (Rom 8:39). I hold fast to your promise: "I will instruct you and teach you in the way you should go; I will counsel you and watch over you" (Psa. 32:8).

Amen.

אֵל שַׁדַּי
El Shaddai
6

The All-Sufficient God

El Shaddai is one of the better known names of God. It (*El Shaddai* or *Shaddai*) occurs 48 times in Scripture, 31 times in the Book of Job alone. In both the KJV and the NIV, the name is translated "God Almighty" (*El Shaddai*) and "the Almighty" (*Shaddai*). I am not sure that "Almighty" does justice to this name, but it is difficult to find a single word to substitute for it. Let's see if we can go deeper.

The Meaning of *Shaddai*

Since we are seeking a term that more accurately depicts this name, we need to follow a slightly different process for this study. As usual the comment comes after the passages and the questions, but we first need to attempt to provisionally ascertain what is conveyed by the name.[1] It means more than "Almighty".

Etymology
Some commentators have suggested that this name is derived from a word meaning "to devastate" or "overpower". Others have linked it with an Akkadian term *shadu,* which means mountain.[2] Neither of these suggested derivations is very satisfying. The idea of strength is already contained in the name *Elohim* or *El*. Linking the name *Shaddai* with 'mountain' seems a long shot. There is no adequate link between the concept "mountain" and the truth conveyed when God reveals himself as *El Shaddai*.

One suggestion does merit closer attention. The Hebrew word for breast is *shad.* The term is used in Scripture to refer to breasts (e.g. Psa 22:9; Song of Songs 1:13; 8:1; Isa 32:12; Ezek 23:21). Bear in mind that in the thought of the Israelites the breasts symbolised provision and care, as is evident in Isaiah 66:10-11,

> Rejoice with Jerusalem
> and be glad for her,
> all you who love her;
> rejoice greatly with her,
> all you who mourn over her.
> For you will nurse and be satisfied
> at her comforting breasts;
> you will drink deeply
> and delight in
> her overflowing abundance.

Usage and Context
The best way to ascertain the meaning of the name is to examine the instances in Scripture where it is used. The ideas of blessing, care, provision, faithfulness and protection are uppermost when the name is mentioned. *Shaddai* is infinitely resourceful. We would not expect that these ideas are always to the fore or that no other ideas are present. We are, after all, speaking about God. So *Shaddai* also possesses awesome might; he is to be revered; he is the righteous judge (Job 8:3; 21:20; Psa 68:14; Isa 13:6; Ezek 1:24). But *the primary picture that emerges is of a God of infinite resourcefulness and tenderness, who is faithful to his word, one who watches over his children and delights in imparting the best gifts to them.* We are now in a position to see whether the main passages we study are consistent with this portrayal.

Passages and References

Passages: Gen. 17:1-2; 28:1-5; Ruth 1:19-21; Job 5:17-18; 6:1-4.

References
   Gen. 35:11-12; 43:13; 49:25; **Psa. 91:1-2**; Isa. 49:14-16.

Questions

1. **GENESIS 17:1-2; 28:1-5; 35:11-12.** From these Genesis passages, what provisional conclusions can we come to regarding the meaning of *Shaddai*?

2. **RUTH 1:19-21.** Give *two* reasons why Naomi was so bitter when she returned to Bethlehem?

3.   Imagine that we were able to interview Naomi shortly before her death, and we commiserated with her over the terrible loss she suffered in Moab. What do you think she might say to us about *Shaddai*? (Ruth 2:19-23)

4. Suppose there had been a post-mortem interview with Naomi shortly after Solomon had become king, and the interviewer commented on what a rough life she'd had. How do you think she might have responded? (Ruth 4:13-22)

5. **JOB 6:1-4.** Sitting on the dung-heap with his three "comforters", Job was an extremely unhappy man. He'd suddenly lost everything including his children and his health, and he knew nothing about Satan's accusation or his future restoration. What do you think was his *main* problem?

6. **PSALM 91:1-2.** Note the juxtaposition of the divine names in this psalm. If this statement does not guarantee freedom from adversity (and it doesn't), why would we find it encouraging?

7. In view of what the above passages tell us about *Shaddai*, do you agree that the title "Almighty" doesn't really do justice to the name? If so, what name would you suggest?

Comment

Faithfulness

Our first introduction to *El Shaddai* is to the one who keeps his promises. When God called Abram to leave his homeland, his people and his family, he promised that he would make of him a great nation (Gen. 12:1-3). For years Abram and Sarai had no child. God reaffirmed the promise in more specific terms when he later assured Abram that "a son coming from [his] own body would be [his] heir" (Gen. 15:4). The years dragged by and both Abram and Sarai gave up hope. Then, when Abram was 99 (and Sarai just 10 years younger), *Yahweh* appeared to him and said, "I am *El Shaddai*. . . ." There and then God confirmed the covenant.

So, our first introduction to God as *El Shaddai* is in the context of his faithfulness. He stands by his word even when the fulfilment of the promise seems impossible. Subsequently, when God sent Moses to Pharaoh and wished to reveal the import of his name *Yahweh*, he explained, "I am *Yahweh*. I appeared to Abraham, to Isaac and to Jacob as *El Shaddai*, but by my name *Yahweh* I did not make myself known to them" (Exod. 6:2-30). As *El Shaddai* he not only confirmed the covenant with them but watched over them and protected them in Canaan, where they lived as aliens. It's not as though there is discontinuity here. *El Shaddai* and *Yahweh* are different designations for the same God. The name *Yahweh* certainly highlights God's nature as the one who is actively present with his people and committed to the covenant. The name Shaddai draws particular attention to his care, his protection, and his provision.

Blessing and Protection

It was, therefore, natural for Isaac to invoke the name of *El Shaddai* when he committed his son Jacob to his care. Partings can be hard at the best of times. This one was particularly difficult. Isaac was old and blind and thought he would probably never see Jacob again. He knew that he had pronounced the traditional paternal blessing on Jacob and that the promises God had made to Abraham and him would be fulfilled through Jacob's line. His son was going to Paddan Aram, many miles away to find a wife. It must have been a profoundly moving experience as Isaac blessed Jacob and committed him to the grace of God:

> May *El Shaddai* bless you and make you fruitful and increase your numbers until you become a community of peoples. May he give you and your descendants the blessing given to Abraham, so that you may take possession of the land where you now live as an alien, the land God gave to Abraham (Gen. 28:3-4).

Upon Jacob's return to the land, God met with him. Again God revealed his nature as the faithful one who protects and blesses:

> I am *El Shaddai;* be fruitful and increase in number. A nation and a community of nations will come from you, and kings will come from your body. The land I gave to Abraham and Isaac I also give to you, and I will give this land to your descendants after you (Gen. 35:11- 12).

The same thoughts of blessing and protection are present when Jacob pronounces his paternal blessing upon Joseph. In spite of opposition, God had prospered him and would continue to do so. It is interesting that when Jacob pronounces his testamentary blessing on Joseph, he refers to God's abundant provision in these terms:

> Joseph will prosper "because of *Shaddai* who blesses [him]

with blessings of the heavens above,
blessings of the deep that lies below,
blessings of the breast *(shadayim)* and womb"(Gen. 49:25).

This usage has emboldened some preachers to speak of the "mother love of God". We know that humankind was created in the image of God. It was not only Adam who was created in God's image. Whatever aspects of the image of God remain in us are to be found in humankind, male and female:

So God created man in his own image,
in the image of God he created him;
male and female he created them (Gen. 1:27).

Through the fall, the image of God was marred but not entirely obliterated. Here and there we can see glimpses, as imperfect as they are, of the divine image. If we see it anywhere at all, we see it in the instinct of a mother to love unconditionally, to protect at any cost, to sacrifice and to provide for the infant at her breast. It makes one think of the great affirmation of God's faithfulness in Isaiah 49:

But Zion said,
"The LORD has forsaken me,
the LORD has forgotten me."
Can a mother forget the baby at her breast,
and have no compassion on the child she has borne?
Though she may forget, I will not forget you!
See, I have engraved you upon the palms of my hands;
your walls are ever before me (Isa 49:14-16).

Naomi and Job: Misery Exacerbated
Naomi left Bethlehem for Moab, a happily married woman with two

sons (Ruth 1:1). While in Moab, her husband and her two now adult sons died. Her return to Bethlehem caused quite a stir. The women of the town exclaimed, "Can this be Naomi?" Her response was highly significant.

> "Don't call me Naomi ('My Delight' or 'Pleasant')," she told them. "Call me Mara ('Bitter'), because *Shaddai* has made my life very bitter. I went away full but the LORD *(Yahweh)* has brought me back empty. Why call me Naomi? The LORD *(Yahweh)* has afflicted me; *Shaddai* has brought affliction upon me" (Ruth 1:20-21).

Can you hear the pain in Naomi's voice? It's bad enough to lose your husband and your two sons. But if our affliction is deemed to have come from *Shaddai,* the one who protects and watches over us with tender love, we can understandably feel hopeless and bitter.

We encounter the same thought in Job. Here was a righteous man who served God with all his heart and enjoyed prosperity. Then, suddenly and without warning, his entire world crashed down around his ears. He lost not only his possessions but his children and his health. *We,* as the readers, are given an insight into what was going on behind the scenes. But the first *he* knew about it was when his servants came running from every direction to deliver one element of bad news after another. He sits on the dunghill, full of sores, and yet clinging steadfastly to his faith. Then three of his friends, the notorious "Job's comforters" arrived. They appeared to be comforting him but added insult to his injury by insinuating that he must have been guilty of secret sin to have suffered so much. So Eliphaz, the oldest of the three, trots out truisms in defence of God, or so he thinks: "Blessed is the man whom God corrects," he says, "so do not despise the discipline of *Shaddai"* (Job 5: 17).

In answer to his insensitive friends, Job pours out his complaint. At the heart of his anguish was the fact that he could no longer understand God. What he was experiencing was contradicting all he knew about God. He knew God as *El Shaddai*. And, as was later stated, *"Shaddai* is beyond our reach and exalted in power; in his justice and great righteousness, he does not oppress" (Job 37:23). But Job was experiencing oppression that was almost unbearable. He explained why his pain was so intense:

> If only my anguish could be weighed
> and all my misery placed on the scales!
> It would surely outweigh the sand of the seas –
> No wonder my words have been impetuous.
> The arrows of *Shaddai* are in me,
> My spirit drinks in their poison;
> God's terrors are marshalled against me (Job 6:1-4).

Like Naomi, Job could not grasp how *Shaddai* could turn against him.

In times of danger, the name *El Shaddai* is of particular significance. It must have been a real comfort to know that God, who is sovereign *(El Elyon)*, cares for us more than a mother cares for her children *(Shaddai)*:

> He who dwells in the shelter of **Elyon** (the Most High)
> will rest in the shadow of **Shaddai** (the Almighty).
> I will say of **Yahweh** (the LORD),
> "He is my rock and my fortress,
> my God *(Elohim)*
> in whom I trust" (Psa. 91:1, 2).

In times of rejoicing we may praise him as *El Shaddai,* the compassionate God who protects us and watches over us, who blesses us and provides for us. At the great turning points in our journey, when we embark upon a new career, when we bid farewell to a loved one or undertake a difficult task, when we are apprehensive or afraid; when we are perplexed or when the hurt is so intense that we feel like changing our name to Mara, *we can remember that he is and always remains El Shaddai.*

Most importantly, all God's promises and all his blessings come to us through Jesus (Rom 8:31; 1 Cor 1:30-31; 2 Cor 1:20; Eph 1:3-7; Col 2:9-10). Nowhere do we see the heart of *Shaddai* more clearly than in the love of the one who purchased us with his own blood (Acts 20:28; 1 Pet 1:18-19).

In a Nutshell

A Summary
The name *El Shaddai* (God Almighty) or *Shaddai* (the Almighty) depicts God as more than all-powerful. He is the one who blesses and provides for his children. He watches over us and protects us. He is the All-sufficient One. The ideas of affection and protection are implied in a number of the passages we have consulted. In others, the very fact that *Shaddai* has allowed the affliction serves to intensify the pain. When a loving parent chastens a child it often hurts more than the harsh action of a callous disciplinarian.

Is *Shaddai* almighty? Of course he is. But is that the primary connotation of the title? I don't think so. But when the might and majesty conveyed by the name *El* is combined with the compassion and care conveyed by the term *Shaddai*, we have reason for confidence: "He who dwells in the shelter of **Elyon** will rest in the shadow of **Shaddai**" (Psa. 91:1).

A Prayer

El Shaddai, faithful and compassionate God, you keep your promises and watch over us in the good times and the bad. We bow before you in reverence and gratitude. We are grateful that we are not at the mercy of a blind fate. We also know that even the forces of darkness need your permission to afflict us.

Sometimes we are aware that you are watching over us. You provide for us and bless us. You have blessed us with every spiritual blessing in Christ. You have made us co-heirs with your Son. We know that we are now your children and that it has not yet been made known what we shall be; we also know that we shall be like him for we shall see him as he is. How we look forward to that day!

At other times we are tempted to feel that you have forgotten us. We are reminded that although Isaac committed Jacob to the mercies of *El Shaddai*, Jacob's life was anything but easy. Yet your hand was upon him and your blessing was evident in his life. Whatever trials we face, may we, like Jacob and Joseph and Naomi and Job, experience your goodness and praise your name.

Gracious Father, we know it is in your heart to bless your children and you are all-sufficient. We gladly submit to your gracious will. May the assurance that comes to us spur us on to good works so that we bring honour to your name.

Amen.

NOTES

[1]The procedure for doing this is as follows: (1) we ask if there are any etymological clues, (2) we examine all the passages in which the name *El Shaddai* (or *Shaddai*) is used, and (3) we see if there are recurrent connotations in these passages. This is not as simple as it sounds since we know that the name was used more frequently than *Yahweh* during the time of the patriarchs and each particular reference to *Shaddai* refers to God, who always possesses all of his attributes. Nevertheless I think a picture does emerge.

[2]Akkadian was a language spoken in ancient Mesopotamia.

אֵל עוֹלָם
El Olam
7

The Everlasting God

Before the mountains were born
or you brought forth the whole world,
from everlasting to everlasting (*olam ad olam*)
you are God (Psalm 90:2).

The word *olam* occurs over four hundred times in the Hebrew Bible. It has been translated "eternal", "everlasting", "forever", "lasting", "for all time", and "always". It conveys the thought of permanence as opposed to transience. The title *El Olam* seldom occurs (Gen.. 21: 33; Isa. 40:28; cf. Deut. 33:27; Psa. 90:2; Hab. 1:12) but the word *olam* is often used in the same sentence as God's name to describe the permanence of his promises, his covenant, and his kingdom. It is clear enough that God is eternal; what we need to ascertain is the *spiritual* significance of this foundational truth.

Passages and References

Passages: Gen. 21:22-34; Isa 40:27-31

References
    Deut. 33:27; 2 Chron. 20:21 (cf. Psa. 136), Psa. 90:1-2; 102:11-12; 103:11-18; 138:8; **Dan. 7:13-14** (this passage is in Aramaic); Isa. 51:6; Rom. 16:25, 26; 2 Tim. 1:8-10; **James 1:17; 1 Pet. 1:20**; Jude 24-25; **Rev. 1:8; 10:5-6; 22:13**.

Questions

1. Attempt to explain the concept of eternity to an eight-year-old. Keep it that simple!

2. Do you think that there is a *moral* component to the references to God as the Eternal (Everlasting) God? Do these references convey anything about God besides the fact that he lives forever (e.g. Deut. 33:27; 2 Chron. 20:21; Psa. 103:17; Isa. 51:6)? If so, what truth(s) do they convey?

3. **GENESIS 21:22-34.** Abraham planted a tamarisk tree and called on the name of *El Olam* after he and Abimelech had entered into a covenant. Why do you think he honoured God as *El Olam* at this point?

4. **ISAIAH 40: 27-31.** What are the implications *for us* of the fact that *Yahweh* is *El Olam* (the LORD is the Everlasting God)?

5. There are New Testament passages that celebrate God's constancy and the assurance this gives us regarding our salvation (e.g. Rom. 8:28-39; 1 Pet. 1:3-9). How does the fact that God is *El Olam* provide the ultimate basis for our assurance?

Comment

The Essential Meaning of the Term

As stated above, when the term *olam* is used in relation to human beings it usually denotes permanence. If a Hebrew slave chose not to accept his freedom but to become the permanent possession of a gracious master he would have his ear pierced to show that he wished to serve that master for the rest of his life. The service was no longer temporary but life-long or *olam* (Ex. 21:6). Similarly, Hannah presented her son Samuel to the Lord saying: "I will take him and present him before the LORD, and he will live there always (*ad olam*)". The thought is clear: Samuel was not paying a visit; from then on this was going to be his permanent abode (1 Sam. 1:22).

Olam in Relation to God

The first reference to God as *El Olam* occurs in Genesis 21 and almost takes us by surprise. For some time Abimelech, the Philistine king of Gerar had observed Abraham's prosperity. He saw the necessity, both for himself and his descendants, of establishing cordial relationships. The two men swore an oath to one another. The treaty was to be permanently binding between the descendants of Abraham and those of Abimelech. But why did Abraham plant a commemorative tree and "[call] on the name of the LORD *(Yahweh)*, the Eternal God *(El Olam)*" at the conclusion of this covenant? Why did it seem appropriate that, having entered into a solemn agreement involving trust, Abraham should worship God as *El Olam?*

This incident was no doubt important to Abraham. If ever a man had reason to feel that he was transient, Abraham did. He was living in the land of promise but he was living in tents as an alien (Acts 7:5; Heb 11:8-10). His hope was grounded in God, the God "who calls things that are not as though they were" (Rom. 4:17). He had learned to trust in God, and in God alone, for the fulfilment of the promises. Now one of the powerful local kings recognizes the permanence of the Abrahamic family in the land ("God is with you in everything you do" [Gen. 21:22]) and sees the importance of making a treaty with him. The thought of God's constancy, his faithfulness, must surely have been in Abraham's mind. So it was appropriate that he worship the *Eternal* God who had remained true to his promises.

God's Eternality

On the surface of things, when the word *olam* is used in relation to God it refers to the fact that there was neither beginning nor end to his existence. He "is and was and is to come" (Rev 1:8). He is the great "I AM" (Exod 3:14). But there is more to God's eternality than endlessness. In fact, this is a truth that engages both our minds and our hearts.

A truth that engages our minds. The thought of God's eternality boggles our minds. If we ponder it, we run into a mental wall. We wonder why it should be that God has just always been there.

Here's a suggestion. We certainly can't explain why God should always have existed, but I think we can at least appreciate why we can't explain God's "origin". An (admittedly limited) illustration may help. In this information age, our personal computers perform a whole host of complicated functions with ease, so much so that some almost attribute intelligence and personality to these machines. The key is in the programming. We may not like the comparison but, in a sense, we too have been "programmed". We are certainly not just automatons but our minds are wired to live in a finite world. An important part of this wiring is the notion of cause and effect. We know, almost instinctively, that every effect has to have a cause (quantum mechanics notwithstanding). This law applies to everything we know--*in the finite world,* that is. And when we attempt to cross over into the infinite realm, our minds protest: God cannot just always have been there. He too must have been "caused." We cannot cope with the concept of an eternally existing person, not because the idea is inherently defective, but because our minds tell us God must also have been caused. But, as Kenneth Hemphill states, "We have been taught that everything that exists has to have a prior cause. . . . God is the uncaused cause. He is the first cause and before him there was no other and after him there will be no other. Life is found in him."[1]

It may be difficult or impossible to get our minds around the idea of God's eternality, but the *alternative is even more problematic.* Given the fact of our own existence, it is particularly difficult to conceive of an "eternal nothingness," and to imagine that nothing gave rise to something.

No attempt is made in Genesis 1 to explain God's existence. The Writer to the Hebrews declares simply: "Anyone who comes to (God) must believe that he exists and that he rewards those who earnestly seek him" (Heb. 11:6). Let's take this one step further. If God, and only God, is eternal, there is no such thing as "eternity" as an abstract entity apart from God. This emboldened Karl Barth to say:

It is the living God himself. It is not only a quality which he possesses. It is not only a space in which he dwells. . . . We cannot for one moment think of eternity without thinking of God, nor can we think of it otherwise than by thinking of God. . . . Eternity is the living God himself.[2]

That means that we may not look on eternity as a uniform, grey sea before, above and after time. Eternity is more than time with the ends knocked out. We are thinking of a different dimension of reality. God, who alone is eternal, brought time and space into being. The subject boggles our finite minds, and so it should. We are discussing *El Olam* - the Eternal God. But the emphasis in Scripture is not on a quasi-philosophical discussion about the nature of eternity. The eternality of God has important spiritual implications.

A truth that encourages our hearts. From a biblical point of view, the notion of God's eternality has far less to do with how long God has lived or will live than with his character. Because he is eternal, he is dependable; he is consistent; he is faithful. He is not subject to the changes associated with time and degeneration. That, in essence, is what is meant by passages such as Malachi 3: 6, "I, the LORD, do not change," and James 1: 17, "Every good and perfect gift is from above, coming down from the Father of heavenly lights, who does not change like shifting shadows." Again Barth gives us a glimpse into the spiritual significance of the concept: "Rightly understood, the statement that God is eternal tells us what God is, not what He is not. . . . As the eternal One he is present personally at every point of our time. As the eternal One it is he who surrounds our time and rules it with all that it contains."[3]

The passages in which God is declared to be eternal refer to far more than the duration of his existence. When he is recognized and worshipped as *El Olam*, it is his character that is in mind. His eternality is celebrated when his people feel that they are adrift on an uncertain sea. This concept is certainly present when the Psalmist cries out in distress:

My days vanish like smoke;
my bones burn like glowing embers . . .
My days are like the evening shadow;
I wither away like grass.

But you, O LORD, sit
enthroned forever *(l'olam);*
Your renown endures
through all generations.
You will arise and have
compassion on Zion,
for it is time to show favour to her;
The appointed time has come (Psa. 102:11-12).

God's eternality implies his unfailing faithfulness.

Lord *(Adonai),* you have been our dwelling place
throughout all generations.
Before the mountains were born
or you brought forth the earth and the world,
from everlasting to everlasting *(olam ad olam)*
you are God *(El)* (Psa. 90: 1-2).

We can hardly find a greater psalm of praise than Psalm 103:

For as high as the heavens are above the earth,
so great is his love for those who fear him;
as far as the east is from the west,
so far has he removed our transgressions from us.

As a father has compassion on his children,
so the LORD has compassion on those who fear him;
for he knows how we are formed,
he remembers that we are dust.
As for man his days are like grass,
he flourishes like a flower of the field;
the wind blows over it and it is gone,
and its place remembers it no more.

But from everlasting (*olam*) to everlasting (*olam*)
the LORD'S love is with those who fear him. . . . (Psa. 103:11-17).

Two important implications

In the first place, we *can have absolute certainty regarding the future.* The eternal God has an eternal purpose--a purpose which is as certain as his nature. Your salvation and mine are rooted in eternity. Peter tells us that we were redeemed "with the precious blood of Christ, a lamb without blemish and defect." He adds:

He was chosen before the creation of the world, but was revealed in these last times for your sake (I Pet. 1: 18-20).

Paul makes it clear to us that "(God) chose us in Christ before the creation of the world" (Eph. 1:4). Think of the import of these words:

Those God foreknew he also predestined to be conformed to the likeness of his Son, that he might be the firstborn among many brothers. And those he predestined, he also called; those he called, he also justified; those he justified, he also glorified (Rom. 8:29-30).

These truths should really inspire us. And though we are grateful for what he has revealed to us, we ought not to make a futile attempt to go back into eternity and take up our position behind God so that we can see over his omniscient shoulder and discern his purpose in intricate detail. We can only stand where we are, in time, as those who have undeservedly experienced his grace. But we realize, according to these and other passages, that God did not one day discover to his surprise that you had decided to give your life to him. Your salvation is rooted in God's eternity.

And in the second place, we not only find hope for the future; we *derive strength now.* Earlier we were struck by Psalm 90: 1-2:

Lord, you have been our dwelling place
throughout all generations.
Before the mountains were born
Or you brought forth the
earth and the world,
from everlasting to
everlasting
You are God.

There is another passage that spells out what our relationship with the Eternal One can do for us here and now:

Why do you say, O Jacob,
and complain, O Israel,
"My way is hidden from the LORD *(Yahweh);*
my cause is disregarded by my God *(Elohim)"?*

Do you not know?
Have you not heard?

The LORD *(Yahweh)* is the everlasting God *(Elohim Olam)*,
The Creator of the ends of the earth.
He will not grow tired or weary,
and his understanding no one can fathom.
He gives strength to the weary
and increases the power of the weak.
Even youths grow tired and weary,
and young men stumble and fall;
but those who hope in the LORD *(Yahweh)*
will renew their strength.
They will soar on wings like eagles;
they will run and not grow weary,
they will walk and not be faint (Isa. 40:28-31).

When we are struck by the fleeting nature of life; when we experience disappointment or disillusionment or fatigue; when we struggle through the night of time with its contradictions and its reversals; then we can thank God that, even in time, we know him as *El Olam*--the Eternal God. We rejoice that the One who was chosen before the foundation of the world, was revealed in these last days for our sakes (I Pet. 1:20). We remember that he said, "Before Abraham was, I AM" (John 8:58). We know that "he is the same yesterday, today and forever" (Heb. 13:8). He is "the Alpha and the Omega, the First and the Last, the Beginning and the End" (Rev. 22:13; cf. 1:8, 17).

When nothing around us seems constant, we can know: "The LORD is the everlasting God *(Elohay Olam Yahweh)*. . . . Those who hope in the LORD will renew their strength" (Isa. 40:28, 31).

To him who is able to keep you from falling
and present you before his glorious presence

without fault and with great joy -
to the only God, our Saviour
be glory, majesty, power and authority,
through Jesus Christ our Lord,
before all ages, now and for evermore (emphasis added). Amen
(Jude 24, 25).

In A Nutshell

A Summary
When it refers to mankind, the word *olam* emphasizes permanence as opposed to transience. It can mean lifelong. When it refers to *God* or is linked to the name *El,* it conveys the idea that he is eternal. But when we say God is eternal, we mean more than that he lives forever or is uncreated. We also understand that he is perfectly consistent and reliable. It was probably this idea that was in Abraham's mind when he planted a tamarisk tree and called on the name of *Yahweh, El Olam* (Gen. 21:33). The knowledge of God's faithfulness and Abimelech's recognition of God's blessing was a reminder to Abraham of the faithfulness of the LORD, the Everlasting God. The fact that God is *El Olam* certainly gives us assurance for the future, and it also inspires (and energizes) us in the present.

A Prayer

El Olam, Eternal God, your steadfast love endures forever. We trust in your promises because you are the eternal God. We change but you remain the same. Your word is sure because you are perfect and you never change. "Your love, O LORD, reaches to the heavens, your faithfulness to the skies. Your righteousness is like the mighty mountains, your justice like the great deep. . . . How priceless is your unfailing love (*chesed*)! Both high and low find refuge in the shadow of your wings" (Psa. 36:5-7).

LORD, nothing in this life is permanent. We are sometimes bewildered by the pace of change. But we rest in your unfailing love. And we rejoice in the certainty only you provide. We pray that you will sanctify us through and through, that our whole spirit and soul and body will be kept blameless at the coming of our Lord Jesus Christ. And we rejoice in the assurance of your dependable word: "The one who calls you is faithful and he will do it" (1 Thess 5:23-24). We thank you Lord for a foundation that can never be shaken. Our hope is in you O LORD, the Everlasting God. Our prayer is that you will enable us to be steadfast, immovable, always abounding in the work of the Lord. Amen.

NOTES

[1]Kenneth Hemphill, *The Names of God* (Nashville, TN: Broadman and Holman Publishers, 2001), 66.

[2]Karl Barth, *Church Dogmatics,* ed. G. W. Bromiley, and T. F. Torrance, vol. 2, *The Doctrine of God*, pt. 1, trans. T. H. L. Parker, W. B. Johnston, Harold Knight, and J. L. M. Haire (Edinburgh: T & T Clark, 1957), 638.

[3]Ibid., 613.

יְהוָה יִרְאֶה
Yahweh Yireh
8

The LORD Will Provide

So far we have considered the meaning of the names, *Elohim*, *Yahweh*, and *Adonai* as well as the compound names of God that are formed by combining a concept with the word *El*. We now give our attention to the names of God that are formed by using a word in combination with *Yahweh*. Three matters need to be re-emphasized: (1) when a word is used in conjunction with *Yahweh*, all that is contained in the name *Yahweh* is conveyed by the name; the attached term does not introduce an entirely new concept, but highlights a particular aspect of God's nature; (2) the "Comment" comes after the "Passage(s)", the "References," and the "Questions" so that the study is inductive; we interact with the passages themselves *before* considering some commentary on it; and (3) we do not have to answer every question; the questions are intended to make us think and to stimulate discussion; they are not an end in themselves.

Passage and References

Passage: **Gen. 22:1-19** (cf. Heb. 11:17-19) **Rom. 8:31-32**.

References
   Gen. 3:7, 21; Deut. 28:11-13; Isa. 53:10; Rom. 3:25-26; 2 Cor. 9:8, 11; Phil. 4:19; Rev. 22:1, 2, 17.

Questions

1. Have you ever sung the song, "Jehovah Jireh"? (I have, and I enjoyed it). The lyrics celebrate the fact that "My God shall supply all my need, according to his riches in glory," and conclude with the emphatic declaration, "Jehovah Jireh cares for me, for me, for me."[1] How did *you* like it? It is not clever to be pedantic about songs of praise, but consider three matters:

(1) What is the central thrust of this song?

(2) Is the song God-centered or "me" centered?

(3) From what you read in the passages above, do you think the song does justice to the concept conveyed by the name *Yahweh Yireh* (*Jehovah Jireh*)?

2. What made God's bizarre-sounding instruction to Abraham particularly poignant and relevant (Gen. 22:1-2)?

3. Abraham acted in faith (he had not always done so in the past). There is not the slightest hint of hesitation. According to the writer to the Hebrews, he was convinced that if he sacrificed Isaac, Isaac could not remain dead (Heb. 11:17-19). Do you think he felt any emotion on the journey, and when he tied his son and placed him on the altar? The text doesn't say, so why do you think so (or not)?

4. When Abraham told the servants that he and Isaac would worship and then *they* would return, do you think he was buying time, or did he mean it? Why?

5. When Abraham told Isaac that "God himself [would] provide a lamb for the burnt offering," was he fobbing Isaac off or did he really believe it? What makes you think this?

6. Think of how "lonely" Abraham must have been. He could not share what he was about to do with anyone until the critical moment; not Sarah, not his servants, not even Isaac. Have you ever been placed in a position of "loneliness" during a trial, a time when you could not share with anyone what you were doing or why you were doing it?

7.   Once this incident was over, do you think it had any impact on the relationship between Abraham and Isaac? If so, what do you think it did (1) for Abraham, and (2) for Isaac (if we do the math, Isaac would not have been a child at the time)?

8.   We know that God, who provided a lamb as a substitute for Isaac, provided *the* Lamb as a substitute for us (Isa. 53:5-7; John 1:29, 36; Rom 3:25; 1 Pet. 1:18-19; 2:24-25; Rev. 5:6-10). So, when we speak of *Yahweh Yireh*, what is primarily in mind? Is this not a whole lot better than the somewhat distorted notion that the Almighty exists to provide our "wants"?

9.   Having established the fact that *Yahweh Yireh's* primary provision is for our most essential need, and was made at great cost to himself, is it legitimate to believe that he will provide all our other "needs"? Could we say that God is concerned with the single most important issue but leaves the less significant details to us? "He helps those who help themselves." On what do you base your answer? (Rom. 8:31-32; 2 Cor. 9:8)

10. Of course, in a general sense, God provides our needs by creating normal opportunities (e.g. a job, the strength to work). But can you recount a time in your life when God did indeed provide your needs

in such a way that it strengthened your faith ("provision": he saw what you needed even before you asked him and provided [Matt. 6:8])?

Comment

Jehovah Jireh or *Yahweh Yireh* (to be more correct) is probably the best known of the compound names of God. In recent times it has been popularized in the song *"Jehovah Jireh, my Provider."* For years the name was on the front page of the magazine of the China Inland Mission and was inscribed at the entrance of the mission's headquarters in London.

But the best known of the compound names of *Yahweh* is not, strictly-speaking, a name of God. *Yahweh Yireh* is the name that Abraham gave to *a place.* But, when all is said and done, the place where the substitute ram was sacrificed in Isaac's stead is so named because of what God did there, and what God did there was a revelation *par excellence* of his nature. So by a completely valid process, we can call God *Yahweh Yireh* or *Jehovah Jireh.* In fact, when we consider who God is, this name is particularly appropriate.

The Second Most Poignant Incident in Scripture
The incident in which God revealed himself as *Yahweh Yireh* is, in my book, the second most poignant event in Scripture. For a number of years there had been laughter in the home of Abraham and Sarah. God had done the impossible for them and they watched their miracle child grow up before their eyes. Isaac means "he laughs" and

they must often have chuckled as they marvelled at God's goodness to them and his faithfulness to his promise. But, in a moment, God wiped the smile from Abraham's face. There could be no doubt that it was God who was speaking. Abraham knew his voice. And he knew that obedience was the only appropriate response to the voice of God. The command was clear enough even if it did not make sense to him.

> Take your son, your only son, Isaac, whom you love, and go to the region of Moriah. Sacrifice him there as a burnt offering on one of the mountains I will tell you about (Gen 22:2).

Three days is a long time to contemplate how you are going to sacrifice your son. One wonders what thoughts passed through Abraham's mind as he travelled northwards with his beloved son. At last they saw Moriah in the distance and Abraham said to his two servants, "Stay here with the donkey while I and the boy go over there. We will worship and then *we* will come back to you" (22:5; emphasis added).

As the father and son set out with the wood and the earthenware jar containing the fire, Isaac was puzzled and asked the understandable question, "Father . . . the fire and the wood are here, but where is the lamb for the burnt offering?" Abraham's answer must have satisfied Isaac: "God himself will provide a lamb for the burnt offering, my son." This was not just an evasive reassurance to pacify the young man. Abraham did not know how God would do it, but he believed what he was saying. God had promised that Isaac would be born. The impossible had happened once. Abraham knew that all God's promises to him regarding the future were vested in Isaac. The permanent death of Isaac was therefore not a possibility. The Writer to the Hebrews explains:

By faith Abraham, when God tested him, offered Isaac as a sacrifice. He who had received the promises was about to sacrifice his one and only son, even though God had said to him, "It is through Isaac that your offspring will be reckoned." Abraham reasoned that God could raise the dead, and figuratively speaking, he did receive Isaac back from death (Heb. 11: 17 -19).

The critical moment arrived. And this time it was not for Abraham to tamper with the promise in an attempt to bring it within the bounds of possibility. He had done that before with very serious consequences. So he built an altar, arranged the wood on it, bound his son and laid him on the wood. Without delay, he took the knife and raised it to kill his beloved son. In that instant, the Angel of the LORD called out from heaven:

Abraham! Abraham! Do not lay a hand on the boy. Do not do anything to him. Now I know that you fear God, because you have not withheld from me your son, your only son (Gen. 22:11- 12).

As Abraham looked up he saw a ram caught by its horns in a thicket. God *had* provided the lamb for the burnt offering.

The Generous Provider
Abraham called the name of that place: *"Yahweh Yireh* — The LORD will provide." And at the time of the writing of the first five books of Moses, it was still said, "On the mountain of the LORD it will be provided."

The Hebrew verb from which Yireh is derived is *ra'ah*—"to see". The thought being conveyed is that God sees the future as well as the past and the present and is therefore able to provide exactly what is needed. Significantly the English word "provision" is made up of two Latin words that mean "to see beforehand".[2]

From the very beginning, God has been a God of provision. Creation testifies to his bountiful provision. When God created humankind, he said:

I give you every seed-bearing plant on the face of the whole earth and every tree that has fruit with seed in it. They will be yours for food. And to all the beasts of the earth and all the birds of the air and all the creatures that move on the ground — everything that has the breath of life in it — I give every green plant for food. God saw all that he had made and it was very good (Gen. 1 :29-31).

When mankind fell God came looking for Adam and Eve. No sooner had God pronounced judgment on them than he provided for their immediate need: "The LORD God made garments of skin for Adam and his wife and clothed them" (Gen. 3:21). After the flood God promised to bless Noah and to provide for him (Gen. 9:1-7). He provided liberally for Abraham, Isaac and Jacob.

His assurance to Israel again reveals his generosity. His promise was, of course, contingent upon their obedience:

The LORD will grant you abundant prosperity. . . . The LORD will open the heavens, the storehouse of his bounty, to send rain on your land in season and to bless all the work of your hands. You will lend to many nations but will borrow from none. The LORD will make you the head, not the tail. If you pay attention to the commands of the LORD your God that I give you this day and carefully follow them, you will always be at the top, never at the bottom (Deut. 28:11-13).

We celebrate this fact every time we recite the 23rd Psalm: "The LORD is my Shepherd, I shall not be in want. . . ."(Psa. 23:1).

Future Abundance
The prophets look forward to a time of abundant provision when God restores his people (Micah 4:4; Zech 3:10). The same thought recurs in the New Testament:

> God is able to make all grace abound to you, so that in all things at all times, having all that you need you will abound in every good work. . . . You will be made rich in every way so that you can be generous on every occasion (2 Cor. 9:8, 11).

He assures the Philippians in categorical terms: "My God will meet all your needs according to his glorious riches in Christ Jesus" (Phil 4:19). At the end of Scripture we again see God as *Yahweh Yireh*. There we encounter the same big-hearted generosity.

> Then the angel showed me the river of the water of life, as clear as crystal, flowing from the throne of God and the Lamb down the middle of the great street of the city. On each side of the river stood the tree of life, bearing twelve crops of fruit, yielding its fruit every month. And the leaves of the tree are for the healing of the nations (Rev. 22:1-2).

> The Spirit and the bride say, "Come!" And let him who hears say, "Come!" Whoever is thirsty, let them come; and whoever wishes, let them take of the free gift of the water of life (Rev. 22:17).

More to this Name than We Realize

One sometimes hears Christians celebrating the fact that God is *"Jehovah Jireh*, my provider." They rejoice in the knowledge that God can provide all their need according to his riches in glory. We ought never to discourage any believer who is genuinely looking to God to provide their need, but sadly some focus more on the provision than on the Provider. If that is where the accent is, we are thinking of God as a means to an end. The truth is far more wonderful than that.

God's capacity to provide is not just an aspect of his character. When God spoke to Abraham, he told him not to lay a hand on Isaac. As he looked up, Abraham saw the substitute in the thicket. I said that this incident was, to my mind, the *second* most poignant in the Bible. There is only one that is more moving. Years later, another drama was enacted less than a kilometre from that very spot on Mount Moriah. There, at the Place of the Skull, another Father was about to sacrifice his one and only Son, whom he loved. As one writer put it, "The demand that rang through the soul of Abraham out there on those Canaanite hills was but an echo of the greater demand made by God upon himself out there on those everlasting hills — a demand met within sight of Moriah itself."[3]

On that occasion there was no voice to put a stop to the proceedings. There was no one above or behind God to stay the execution. *Yahweh Yireh* was making his ultimate provision.

> What, then, shall we say in response to this? If God is for us, who can be against us? He who did not spare his own Son, but gave him up for us all - how will he not also, along with him, graciously give us all things? (Rom 8:31- 32).

God's ultimate provision was not the ram caught in the thicket but the Lamb without spot or wrinkle, the Lamb of God who takes away the sin of the world. Everything we ever receive from God's hand is on account of him. It is far more comprehensive than the supply of this or that need. Every one of his gifts comes to us through Jesus and therefore at an inestimably great cost to him. The place, *Yahweh Yireh* is the place where God provided a substitute. As *Yahweh Yireh,* he did not spare his own Son but delivered him up for us all. When I remember that, I can never take *any* of his gifts for granted.

In A Nutshell

Summary

The name *Yahweh Yireh* celebrates God's nature as the ultimate Provider. We sell ourselves short if we limit his provision to our wants or even to this or that need. The context in which the name was revealed points to the provision of God's greatest gift to us.

From the very outset, God has provided. That is because he *has* provision (he sees beforehand). He saw the great need that Abraham had; he had already provided a lamb for the burnt offering. He had anticipated our great need even before the fall: Christ was the "Lamb without blemish and defect chosen before the creation of the world but was revealed in these last times for [our] sake" (1 Pet. 1:19-20). Paul can therefore pose the rhetorical question, "He who did not spare his own Son, but gave him up for us all—how will he not also, along with him, graciously give us all things?" (Rom. 8:32)

A Prayer

LORD, you know what we need before it even comes into our minds. You are *Jehovah Jireh*. At the point of Isaac's greatest need, you intervened. And you have gone to huge lengths to provide for our salvation. Why, at times, do we find it so hard to believe that you will provide our every need and that even when you withhold our wants, it is for our good? You are the same LORD who provided for Abraham and Isaac. O LORD, please help us to learn to trust you as fully and as simply as Abraham did and to worship you as our *Yahweh Yireh*.

Amen.

NOTES

---

[1] Jehovah Jireh
My provider
His grace is sufficient
For me, for me, for me
Jehovah Jireh
My provider
His grace is sufficient for me

My God shall supply all my needs
According to his riches in glory
He will give His angels
Charge over me
Jehovah Jireh cares
For me, for me, for me
Jehovah Jireh cares for me

[2] Kenneth Hemphill, *The Names of God* (Nashville, TN: Broadman and Holman, 2001), 85; Ann Spangler, *The Names of God* (Grand Rapids, MI: Zondervan, 2009), 28.

[3] I made a careful note of this quotation several decades ago, and attributed it in my note to F. B. Meyer, but have been unable to trace its exact source.

יְהוָה נִסִּי
Yahweh Nissi
9

The LORD My Banner

Do you sometimes feel that you are in a conflict zone? If so, it shouldn't surprise you. From Genesis 3 to Revelation 20, the Bible describes the story of humanity in terms of conflict. And God himself enters the fray. We win the war, but while ultimate victory is assured it is possible for us to lose some battles and suffer heavy casualties along the way. For that reason, it behoves us to take seriously the battle strategy laid down by the Lord himself. This makes the name *Yahweh Nissi* particularly relevant.

Passages and References

Passage: Exod. 17:8-16

References
   Deut. 25: 17-19; 1 Sam. 15: 2-3, 20, 32-33 ; 30:1, 2, 16-19; **2 Sam. 1: 4-10**; Psa. 60:4-6; Isa. 54:17; Zech. 4:6; Rom. 16:21; 2 Cor. 10:3-5; Eph. 4:27; 6:10-12; **1 Pet. 5: 8-11**; Rev. 12:7-9; 13:10; 19:11- 21

Questions

1.   On the surface, we have before us the story of a clash in the desert between the Israelites and a people who felt threatened by

the presence near their territory of a huge migrating company. What is your gut reaction to the Amalekites' attack?

2.   What was the hereditary relationship of the Amalekites to Israel (Gen. 36:12)?

3.   There was a perpetual enmity between the Amalekites and the Israelites, *one recognized and sanctioned by God himself* (Deut. 25:19; 1 Sam. 15:2-3). To this day, this passage is read in the synagogue at the Feast of Purim (celebrating God's deliverance of the Jews in the time of Esther). Any idea why? (Deut. 25:19; 1 Sam. 15: 2-3, 20, 32-33; 2 Sam. 1: 1-16; Esther 3:1, 8, 9; 9:28).

4.   Do you think this was the working out of a grudge or it there more to it than that? If so, why was God so uncompromising in his attitude towards co-existence with the Amalekites?

5.   As we consider our own involvement in the cosmic battle, who or what is symbolized by the Amalekites? (2 Cor. 10:3-5; Eph. 6:10-12; 1 Pet. 5:8-11)

6.   We are not travelling through the Sinai Peninsula and need not fear a physical attack. In what ways could a spiritual battle be waged against us?

7.   Why was there to be absolutely no compromise with the intransigent Amalekites?

8.   In your own words, explain the spiritual significance of Moses' raised hands.

9.   If the "raised hands" represents prayer (trust in *Yahweh*), what does it tell us about the place of prayer in "spiritual warfare"? Of course we cannot extrapolate the incident into a universal principle, but would you go so far as to say that real spiritual victories are only won through the involvement of God?

Comment

Israel had left Egypt and was on her way to Mount Sinai when she got her first taste of post-Exodus opposition. The Amalekites never met the Israelites head on. When the large company of Israelites including women and children was weary and worn out, the Amalekite army came up behind them and attacked the stragglers who were lagging behind. They were a soft target. The Amalekites' strategy was reprehensible, and the situation was exacerbated by the fact that, as descendants of Esau, they were actually close relatives of the Israelites. Whether they liked it or not, the Israelites had a battle on their hands (Exod. 17:8-16; Deut. 25:17-19).

The Cosmic Conflict

Before we survey the strange battle that followed this dastardly attack, it would be helpful to place this incident in the wider context of the cosmic conflict raging in the universe. There is a sense in which we can say that history is a record of the conflict between good and evil. To obtain this perspective on history we only have to look at the beginning and at the end of Scripture. At the beginning we are given a picture of harmony and peace. Mankind is walking with their Creator and all is perfectly well. But the harmony and tranquillity of the garden are soon shattered by a discordant voice: "Did God say . . . ?" Sin and sickness, pain and war, heartache and death enter at this point. Evil becomes a reality in the experience of the race. Since the fall we have never lived without strife.

But at the end of history the tranquillity is gloriously restored:

> I heard a loud voice from the throne saying, "Now the dwelling of God is with men, and he will live with them. They will be his people, and God himself will be with them and be their God. He will wipe every tear from their eyes. There will be no more death or crying or pain, for the old order of things has passed away" (Rev. 21:3-4).

Isaiah and Micah are typical of the Old Testament prophets as they look forward to the day when "nation will not take up sword against nation, nor will they train for war any more" (Isa. 2:4; Micah 4:3).

Between those two events, good and evil are at war. Usually there are surface symptoms such as ambition and greed, jealousy and rival ideologies. We cannot underestimate the role these factors play. But in the final analysis, this is a battle between personalities, not just abstract principles. Every now and again we are given a glimpse of the personalities behind the powers. We see the Ancient Serpent deceiving Eve in the garden (Gen. 3:1-7). We see Satan challenging Job's integrity before God (Job 1-2). We see him accusing Joshua, the High Priest, before the angel of the LORD (Zech. 3). Then there is that amazing glimpse into the powers behind the political order in Daniel, chapter 10. Daniel had been praying for his people and an angelic messenger was sent to him and gives him some insight into a behind-the-scenes cosmic conflict (Dan. 10:12-13, 20-21). We see this again in the Revelation. John describes some important scenes in the cosmic battle (Rev. 12:7-9).

Whatever the precise meaning of the goings-on in the heavenly realms, it appears that behind many of the events on earth there are spiritual principalities at work. A battle is raging. We may only see the odd skirmish, but it is all part of a much bigger war which is raging whether or not we are conscious of it.

When Jesus came to earth, he entered the fray. We hear him saying: "If I drive out demons by the Spirit of God, then the kingdom of God has come upon you. . . . How can anyone enter a strong man's house and carry off his possessions unless he first ties up the strong man?" (Matt. 12:28-29). When the 72 returned expressing joy that the demons were subject to them in Jesus' name, he responded, "I saw Satan fall like lightening from heaven." But he exhorted them to rejoice that their names were written in heaven rather than in the subjugation of the demons to them (Luke 10: 17-22). On the eve of his crucifixion he reminded his disciples that "in this world (they would) have trouble" and added immediately, "But take heart! I have overcome the world" (John 16:33).

The Writer to the Hebrews tells us of the way in which Jesus won his ultimate victory: "(He shared our humanity) so that by his death he might destroy him who holds the power of death — that is, the devil" (Heb. 2: 14). And Paul explains that "having disarmed the powers and authorities, he made a public spectacle of them, triumphing over them by the cross" (Col. 2: 15). The decisive victory has been won. But God's program to eliminate evil must run its course. The outcome is certain but the battle still rages. And every skirmish, whether it is a physical battle with the Amalekites or a mental tussle with an ideology or a principle, must be seen as an episode within the greater war.

An Effective Battle Strategy
In the battle with the Amalekites there are some important lessons about effective battle strategy. Imagine that you are a spectator perched on a hill in the Sinai Peninsula. You are able to observe this huge company making its way through the desert. They are not happy. In that region water and food are scarce and they haven't yet learned that God would never have led them out of Egypt only to abandon them in the desert. You notice that some of the more vulnerable travellers are lagging behind. Evening is about to fall. And then you see the Amalekites attack those at the rear and mow them down mercilessly. The message gets through to Moses and he summons Joshua and instructs him to marshal a make-shift army to fight the Amalekites on the following day. As you watch the battle, you are amazed at the fluctuating fortunes of the Israelites. At times they drive back the Amalekites with relative ease. Then the tide

turns and the Amalekites are successful. Then the Israelites have the upper hand again. And so the fortunes fluctuate.

You then notice that three men are on top of the opposite hill. The central figure is Moses and with him are Aaron and Hur. Moses' hands are raised to heaven as he lifts the staff, which had served as a sign of God's presence in Egypt and at the Red Sea. The Israelites outmatch the Amalekites. Moses' hands tire and he lowers them. But as he does so the tide turns again. This pattern continues. Whenever his hands are raised the Israelites gain the ascendency, but whenever they are lowered the Amalekites are in control.

You then see Aaron and Hur pushing a large stone so that Moses can be seated on it. They stand on either side of him and hold his hands up for several hours. Joshua wins the battle and the Amalekites are forced to flee.

There is a point of major spiritual significance in the account. Moses built an altar and called it *Yahweh Nissi*--the LORD is my Banner. He said, "For hands were lifted up to the throne of the LORD." The Hebrew word rendered "banner" is not easy to translate. The simplest explanation is one that is consistent both with the context and with the language used. The altar was built and named to make one thing crystal clear: *the LORD had granted victory*. It was obvious that Joshua's army was able to gain the upper hand only when Moses' hands were lifted up to the throne of God.

A banner is intended to be a rallying point for an army. It represents what they are fighting for and boosts morale. Hopefully it strikes fear into the enemy as well. In a sense, the sight of Moses at the top of the hill, rod in hand, and arms raised to heaven, was like a banner to the army. But there was more to it than that. The attack had come suddenly. There was no time for any of the customary battle preparations, one of which would possibly have been the erection of a banner. But the attack was an attack on the people of God and Moses was interceding with the LORD for his people. Instead of fighting under a banner which would provide a psychological boost, Israel was fighting under the throne of *Yahweh*. **He** is *Yahweh Nissi*— their unseen banner. What a banner is intended to do, *Yahweh*, in fact, does!

Joshua couldn't think it was his generalship that secured the victory. He knew full well that the Israelites only prevailed when Moses' hands were raised. It was not Moses' prayer, as such (symbolized by his upraised hands) that provided the victory. Moses didn't have the strength to keep his arms raised. Aaron and Hur couldn't take too much credit. All they were doing was to help hold Moses' hands up. Only when hands were lifted up to the throne of God were the Israelites victorious. Clearly, the victory was attributable to him.

Although our focus is upon this particular incident, we have to see it as an episode in an ongoing enmity (Deut. 25:19; 1 Sam. 15:20, 32- 34; Esther 3:1, 8, 9). And that may present a problem to some of us. We have been instructed, in unambiguous terms, to love our enemies (Matt. 5:43-47). Why then was there to be such a ruthless attitude towards the Amalekites? Kenneth Hemphill comments:

When we read such verses we sometimes recoil from the implication of God's command to utterly destroy Amalek, because we do not fully understand the strategy of the enemy. The Amalekites represent the forces of evil as they oppose the work of God and the people of God. The goal of Amalek is to utterly destroy the people of God. When there is compromise with sin, sin does its insidious work to corrupt and ultimately destroy us.[1]

Hemphill points out the irony of the fact that the young man who ultimately bore responsibility for Saul's death was an Amalekite. Jesus urged us to take radical steps to eliminate anything that is likely to trip us up (Matt. 5:28-29). There is too much at stake here! The same principle applies today. To be a believer is to be involved in a war. Paul was in absolutely no doubt about that fact. And his exhortation leaves us in no doubt.

> Be strong in the Lord and in his mighty power. (He reminds us that) our struggle is not against flesh and blood, but against the rulers, against the authorities, against the powers of this dark world and against the spiritual forces of evil in the heavenly realms (Eph. 6:10- 12).

Significantly, he concludes his description of the spiritual armour by urging us to "pray in the Spirit on all occasions with all kinds of prayers and requests. With this in mind be alert and always keep on praying for all the saints" (Eph. 6:18).

The outcome of the war is certain. Paul puts it very simply. He says, "The God of peace will soon crush Satan under your feet" (Rom. 16:20). So does the southern gospel song, "I've read the back of the Book and we win." Through Isaiah, the LORD assures us:

> 'No weapon forged against you will prevail,
> and you will refute every tongue that accuses you.
> This is the heritage of the servants of the LORD,
> And this is the vindication from me,' declares the LORD
> (Isa. 54:17).

Remember, the One who sent us out to make disciples prefaced his commission with the words, "All authority in heaven and on earth has been given to me. . . ." (Matt. 28:18).

The Principle of the Raised Banner
There is, however, a very important principle that has to be observed in every battle we fight. It is the principle of the "Raised Banner". Hands have to be lifted up to the throne of the LORD. Listen to the way this principle is enunciated in 2 Corinthians 10:

Though we live in the world, we do not wage war as the world does. The weapons we fight with are not the weapons of the world. On the contrary, they have divine power to demolish strongholds. We demolish arguments and every pretension that sets itself up against the knowledge of God, and we take captive every thought to make it obedient to Christ (2 Cor 10:3-5).

So, whether we like it or not, we are involved in the war. As long as there is evil in the world, until Satan is permanently confined at the end of the age, it cannot be otherwise. Conflict is inevitable. Victory is, however, assured, for the Lord is our Unseen Banner. We are messengers of his peace. But he, the Prince of Peace, was crucified. We are heralds of the good news, but this good news is an affront to human pride. We do not profess to know everything but we dare to say that we know something that is of critical importance. We do so in an age of relativism, an age in which our message is likely to become increasingly unpopular. We carry no sword but the sword of the Spirit. The weapons of our warfare do, however, have divine power to demolish the strongholds of evil. We are fighting under an invincible ensign, *Yahweh Nissi*—The LORD my (our) Banner.

In A Nutshell

Summary
Just as the Israelites were attacked by a ruthless opponent with an inveterate hatred for the people of God, so we have a brutal opponent. He takes no prisoners. But the Israelites were able to defeat their better-organized opponent. The secret was in the fact that Moses' hands were raised to the throne of God. If this battle symbolizes the cosmic battle in which we are involved, then the raised hands would represent prayer and reliance on the Lord. It seems strange that the raised hands of one man, who seemingly had no part in the battle, should influence its outcome so significantly. But that's exactly what happened.   Other important lessons from the incident include: (1) the need for each of the players to do their part, and (2) the impossibility of compromise with an enemy who is bent on our destruction. But the leading truth in this narrative is that God is *Yahweh Nissi*—the LORD my Banner. "Thanks be to God, who always leads us in triumphal procession in Christ" (2 Cor. 2:14).

A Prayer

Lord, we know that there is no way we can avoid the battle. We also know that our sworn enemy strikes us at our most vulnerable points. We realize that as long as we live we will be in the battle zone. But we also know that the one who is in us is greater than the one who is in the world (1 John 4:4). You tell us to be vigilant but we know we need not be afraid.

We know that in our own strength we are no match for the wiles of the devil. But our trust is in you. We are apt to forget that the battle goes badly when we fight in our own strength and that we prevail when we depend upon you. Remind us, Lord, that you are *Yahweh Nissi*, our Banner and that there is no battle we can't win in your name. When we are inclined to rely upon ourselves, please help us never to forget the battle is the Lord's. All glory and honour belongs to you. You LORD are our banner.

Amen.

NOTE

---

[1] Kenneth Hemphill, *The Names of God* (Nashville, TN: Broadman and Holman Publishers, 2001), 110.

יְהוָה רֹפְאֶךָ
Yahweh Rophecha
10

The LORD Who Heals You

There can be few biblical topics about which there are more unanswered questions than the topic of healing. Opinions range from "name-it-and-claim-it" presumption to "thy-will-be-done" resignation. One of the reasons for the divergence of opinion is the tendency to loosen the link between healing and God. Healing is sometimes seen as something God does for us rather than as the result of fellowship with the one who is *Yahweh Rophecha*—the LORD who heals you. Ironically, the disjunction is often most acute in those who lay emphasis on physical healing in the name of Jesus. As we shall see, we have good reason to look to the LORD for healing, but some approaches are less than helpful.

Passages and References

Passages   **Exod. 15:22-27; Deut. 8:1-5; Jam. 5:13-16.**

References
     Num. 12:1-16; 2 Kings 20:1-11; Psa. 147:3; Mark 1:29-34; Luke 4:14-30; Acts 10:38; 19:11-12.

Questions

1. When you think of divine healing, what is the first thing that comes to mind? Have you ever experienced it yourself or known someone who has?

2. Why do you think that the LORD describes himself as *Yahweh Rophecha* (the LORD who heals you) at this particular point in Israel's journey (Exod 15:27)?

3. Try not to infer too much from one passage. There is a condition here. Does it follow that a believer who is living in obedience will be disease free? Conversely, does it mean that a sick Christian must be living in disobedience?

4. What could be meant by the statement: "The essential thought in healing is *restoration to a state of wholeness and normality*, and this can be spiritual or mental or physical well-being." Do you agree?

5. Why do you think healing played such a big part in Jesus' ministry?

6. What about this statement: "When a person comes to Christ, a process of healing commences in which spiritual, psychological, and sometimes physical healing takes place and God progressively turns our brokenness into wholeness"? Do you agree?

7. Do you believe that God heals today, or was physical healing a special sign associated with Jesus and the preaching of the early church?

8. Which approach seems closest to the biblical position:

"Name it, claim it"	"Resignation"	"Relinquishment"
God has provided healing and it is not his will that any of his children should be sick. It all depends on our faith. Healing is there for the taking but need faith.	We all have to die some day and it is better to be spiritually healthy than physically well. If we are sick we should pray, "Thy will be done," and leave it at that.	We commit ourselves to God in active faith, and accept his verdict. Instead of invoking a formula and seeing "faith" as the trigger that activates the formula, we see it as trust in God.

Please explain the reason for your choice.

Comment

An enacted parable

The circumstances under which the LORD revealed himself as *Yahweh Rophecha* are highly significant. In a way they set the tone for much of what appears subsequently. The Israelites had just passed through the Red Sea. Behind them were some of the most amazing events in history. They had experienced slavery and oppression, but they had seen God deliver them through a series of devastating plagues. Among these plagues were infestations of gnats and locusts and frogs. But the worst plagues were the epidemics that struck the people. The festering boils must have caused real misery. But the *coup de grâce* was the plague that resulted in the death of the firstborn throughout the land.

After the miraculous passage through the Red Sea, there was a great celebration. Moses and the Israelites danced and sang a song of praise to the LORD (Ex. 15:1-2, 11-13). There was excitement and jubilation as Miriam led the women, with tambourines in hand, as they danced for joy (Ex. 15:21).

Nothing is more likely to take the song out of one's heart than three days travel in the hot and arid region of the Sinai Peninsula. Their water bottles, filled before they left Egypt, were now empty. They were tired. They had never travelled in the region and there was no water in sight. There were a lot of them. The anxiety level must have risen towards the end of the second day. By the third day they would have begun to panic. But they controlled themselves and travelled on. Then they came across an oasis. Water at last! When you are that thirsty you don't dilly-dally. I'm sure that those at the front of the company dashed to the water's edge and began to gulp down the water. Can you imagine the gasps of disappointment when they realised that they had discovered brackish water, bitter to the taste and quite undrinkable. The angry complaints began to flow. They directed their anger at Moses asking, "What are we to drink?" Moses cried out to the LORD. And the LORD showed him a piece of wood. He threw it into the water and it immediately became fresh. This was probably the best water they had ever tasted.

Clearly this was an enacted parable. There was nothing in the wood that made the water sweet. The message was clear. God could have ensured that the water was fresh before they arrived. The piece of wood did not change the water's composition. But God chose to "heal" the waters and in so doing he was saying: *"I am not just your Saviour and Deliverer from bondage; I am your Provider and Healer. You needed me to get you out of Egypt and I proved faithful. You need me to sustain you on your journey, and I will remain faithful."*

Then the LORD made a decree for them:

> If you will listen carefully to the voice of the LORD your God and do what is right in his eyes, if you pay attention to his commands and keep all his decrees, I will not bring on you any of the diseases I brought on the Egyptians, for I am *Yahweh Rophecha* (the LORD who heals you).[1]

God demonstrated that he was true to his word. At the end of Israel's period of wandering in the Wilderness, Moses was able to say:

Remember how the LORD your God led you all the way in the desert to humble you and to test you in order to know what was in your heart, whether or not you would keep his commands. . . . Your clothes did not wear out and your feet did not swell during these forty years (Deut. 8:2, 4).

There were some instances where specific healing was needed but this was as a direct result of sin. Miriam was healed of leprosy (Num. 12: 1-16). The Israelites who had been bitten by snakes were healed when they looked at the bronze snake Moses had put up on a pole. This became a type of the life that God gives when in faith we focus our eyes on the One who was lifted up on a cross and crushed the head of the Serpent (Num. 21:4-9; John 3:14-16).

Healing in the Old Testament
There are, of course, other examples of healing in the Old Testament. There was Naaman, the Syrian general, who was cleansed of his leprosy when he obeyed the instruction of the prophet Elisha (2 Kings 5: 1-14). There was King Hezekiah whose life was prolonged for fifteen years when he turned his face to the wall and prayed to the LORD (2 Kings 20:1-11).[2] There is an important observation that we need to make. The word for healing which is used frequently in the Old Testament does not only refer to physical healing. It is also used of psychological and spiritual healing. So we read in Psalm 147:3, "He heals the broken-hearted and binds up their wounds." David cries out: "O LORD, have mercy on me; heal me, for I have sinned against you" (Psa 41:4). The LORD says through the prophet Hosea: "I will heal their waywardness and love them

freely, for my anger has turned away from them" (Hos. 14:4). The essential thought in healing is *restoration to a state of wholeness and normality*, and this can be spiritual or mental or physical well-being. In fact, these aspects of God's healing are often much more closely related than we realize.

The Ministry of Jesus
It was certainly not by accident that healing played such an important role in the ministry of Jesus. The gospels are full of accounts of the healing of the sick. All four Evangelists make it very clear that he healed all kinds of diseases. I am not going to cite specific miracles but I think it would be useful to make three observations. First, we have no record that he ever prayed for anyone who was not healed. True, we cannot argue from silence, but there are accounts in which it is implied that he healed many people with all kinds of ailments, from a fever to paralysis and from leprosy to blindness. Peter told those gathered in the home of Cornelius that "God anointed Jesus of Nazareth with the Holy Spirit and power and he went around doing good and healing all who were under the power of the devil, because God was with him" (Acts 10:38).

It is very clear that the healings were signs.[3] They authenticated the message of Jesus and pointed to his identity as the Messiah. They were not just an exhibition of his power but a demonstration of his love and concern; they were also a result of his compassion. When John the Baptist was in prison, he sent messengers to Jesus with the question: "Are you the one who was to come, or should we expect someone else?" Jesus' reply goes right to the heart of the matter: "Go back and report to John what you hear and see: the blind receive sight, the lame walk, those with leprosy are cured, the deaf hear, the dead are raised, and the good news is preached to the poor" (Matt 11:4-5). He was alluding to two passages in Isaiah (35:5- 6 and 61: 1-2) and, in so doing, giving John the answer he needed.

When Jesus sent out the 12 to spread the good news that God's kingdom had arrived, he gave them power and authority to drive out demons and to heal diseases (Luke 9: 1-2). Later he sent out 72 on a similar mission (Luke 10:9). His instruction was simple: "Heal the sick who are there and tell them, 'The kingdom of God is near you.'"

The Early Church
In the early church physical healing went hand in hand with the proclamation of the gospel. Think of the man at the Beautiful Gate of the temple. He had been crippled from birth yet he was miraculously healed. The people were amazed! The Council members were antagonistic but even they had to acknowledge: "Everybody living in Jerusalem knows that they have done an outstanding miracle, and we cannot deny it" (Acts 4:16). As a result of this healing a huge crowd "came running to them" and Peter was able to proclaim the gospel to them. Comments in Acts 5 lead us to believe that many, many people were healed (Acts 5: 12-16). When Philip was in Samaria, the crowd paid close attention to him because they saw people delivered and paralytics and cripples healed (Acts 8:4-8). Some extraordinary miracles (imagine having to refer to a miracle as "extraordinary"; all miracles are, by definition, extraordinary) took place when Paul was in Ephesus (Acts 19:11-12).

Balance
In the interests of balance, I need to point out that we do come across sick Christians in the New Testament. Paul tells the

Philippians that his fellow-worker, Epaphroditus, was ill and almost died. But God had mercy on him (Phil. 2:27). He refers to his own health problem and acknowledges that God had used it for good. Paul is explicit when he writes to the Galatians, "As you know, it was because of an illness that I first preached the gospel to you. Even though my illness was a trial to you, you did not treat me with contempt and scorn" (Gal. 4:13-14). He mentions to Timothy that he had to leave Trophimus sick in Miletus (2 Tim. 4:20).

Of course, it is possible to argue that these references do not really address the question of whether it is God's will to heal all who are sick or at least all believers who are sick. So, for example, it could be conjectured that Paul was subsequently healed, and stated that Epaphroditus was certainly healed, and that we don't know whether Trophimus was eventually healed or whether it was sin in his life that prevented him from being healed. But these arguments are really without substance. Our opinions ought to be based upon the general tenor of biblical teaching. It is not helpful to cite a few verses, such as Psalm 103:3, "Praise the LORD . . . who heals all your diseases . . ." to make them fit a particular point of view, and to insist that it is always God's will to heal everybody. The problem with the tight and untenable view that no Christian should be (or at least remain) ill is that the inference is invariably drawn that the continued illness is on account of unconfessed sin or a lack of faith. But there is a natural aging process from which we, as believers, are not exempt. We can still love God and know his grace in affliction, bowing to his sovereignty and trusting in his grace.

But if *we* have a problem in regard to healing, it is not that we expect too much, *but that we expect too little*. We accept our ailments or take them to the doctor. The thought of taking them to the Lord may not even cross our minds. James is quite explicit about what we should do if we are sick: "Is anyone of you sick? He should call the elders of the church to pray over him and anoint him with oil in the name of the Lord. And the prayer offered in faith will make the sick person well. . . ." (James 5: 14).

"Resignation" versus "Relinquishment"

In the wider church today there are three major positions on healing. Two of these we can eliminate rather quickly. The third, I would suggest, is the basis on which we should come to the Lord when we are in need of physical or emotional healing.

In the first place there is *the "name it and claim it" approach.* Some believe that every Christian has the right to perfect health. They see physical healing as provided for in the atonement (based largely on a misunderstanding of Isa 53:5). If you are sick, they say, it is either because you have sinned or because you have no faith. This view, as I have suggested, is untenable both from a biblical and an experiential point of view. Others, who hold the same position, do so largely because they feel that it enables us to be positive and to exercise faith. If God has promised our healing and provided for it, then we can boldly claim it. They contend that it is not possible to exercise faith if we can't be absolutely sure that we will be healed.

At the other extreme is the view that, to all intents and purposes, *relegates healing to the past.* In reality, we don't really expect God to heal us. We say, "Thy will be done," but there is such a note of resignation about it, that we practically cancel our prayer.

The third approach is to *recognize that God is Yahweh Rophecha and to come to **him** in faith.* It means that we cast ourselves upon him.

We don't have to accept that it is always his will to heal every person in order to come to him. I remember hearing the true story of a couple whose child became terminally ill. His life was in the balance and they were understandably desperate. They prayed earnestly and many of their Christian friends joined them. They begged like the widow who would give the unjust judge no rest until he heeded her request. But the condition of their little son was unchanged. Eventually they could take it no more. So they "gave him" to the Lord, not in a spirit of passive resignation but in the spirit of active faith. "Lord, you gave him to us and we give him back to you. He is yours. If you want to take him to be with you, that is your prerogative. We would like him to be with us but we surrender him to you. He's yours, Lord." A deep peace settled over them. And from that moment there was a change in his condition. He was healed!

Some have called this the "prayer of relinquishment." There is a world of difference between relinquishment and resignation. Resignation gives up and relinquishment gives over! Resignation is a fatalistic "whatever-will-be-will-be." Relinquishment is trusting God and bowing before his sovereign grace.

To be true there have been other cases of surrender in which healing has not taken place. But such has been the sense of peace that there was no doubt that the Great Physician was present. At times one has almost felt that he was saying a gentle "No" to the request for healing but a certain "Yes" to us all as pilgrims and strangers whose citizenship is in heaven. Paul placed all that happens to us in this life in perspective when he said,

We eagerly await a Saviour from there, the Lord Jesus Christ, who, by the power that enables him to bring everything under his control, will transform our lowly bodies so that they will be like his glorious body (Phil. 3:20-21; cf. Heb. 11:13- 16; I Pet. 2:11-12).

Only then will our healing be complete.

Come!

So what do you do if you discover that you have a serious or even a terminal illness? Don't accept that chronic suffering or death is inevitable. If God is still *Yahweh Rophecha*, he can heal you. So, come to the Great Physician *himself.* Do not seek to invoke some formula. And do not focus on your faith. Rather, throw yourself upon the mercy of the Healer. It does not matter to him whether you have an incurable disease or a minor ailment. He is, after all, God. The "big" things are not big to him. He says, "Cast all your anxiety on [me] for [I] care for you" (1 Pet. *5:7).* Jesus Christ is the same yesterday, today and forever (Heb. 13:8). He still says, "*Yahweh Rophecha* - I am the LORD who heals you."

In A Nutshell

Summary

At an important point in their journey from Egypt to Sinai, God promised the Israelites that if they obeyed him they would suffer none of the diseases that had come upon the Egyptians. He declared, "I am *Yahweh Rophecha*—the LORD who heals you."

Healing in Scripture is a more inclusive concept than physical healing. There is sometimes relationship between sin and sickness but it is incorrect to argue for a direct "you-are-suffering-because-you-sinned" relationship. It is not correct to infer that if a Christian is sick and remains sick after prayer, it is because there is sin in their life or they have not exercised faith.

Jesus himself is the Great Physician. And he still heals today. If he does not heal everybody, what approach should we take: "assertive faith," "resignation," or "relinquishment"? We believe that the third approach is the correct one. We should come to him with our physical ailments. Healing ought to be part of the church's evangelistic ministry. We may not agree with all that takes place in the name of divine healing, but we have good reason to believe that healing is very much part of God's nature and of his plan for us.

A Prayer

Lord, you are the Great Physician. And we are in need of healing in so many ways. We confess that sin has taken its toll on us and we feel our brokenness. It is your nature to restore and heal. You are *Yahweh Rophecha*. For that reason we come to you directly.

We thank you Lord for the body's capacity to heal itself. We thank you for those substances in nature that help to bring healing to us and for medical science. But Lord we know that, in the final analysis, you are the healer whether you use natural means or heal by touching us directly.

Father, we pray that you will raise up ministries of healing, ministries devoid of showmanship and pretence, ministries that point to your grace and confirm the word of salvation. And help *us* to trust you as *Yahweh Rophecha*.

We thank you for the ultimate healing and restoration that are ours through our Redeemer. We look forward to the day when "there will be no more death or mourning or crying or pain for the old order of things [will have] passed away" (Rev. 21:4). Right now our lives are in your hands. We gratefully acknowledge that you are indeed *Yahweh Rophecha*.

Amen.

NOTES

[1]You may have heard the name without the pronominal suffix, *Yahweh Rophē* or *Jehovah Rapha*. In this form, the word conveys the same essential thought: it is *Yahweh* who heals. I am simply reproducing the words of our main text: *Yahweh Rophecha*.

[2] We cannot say that if Hezekiah had not "twisted God's arm," his wicked son Manasseh would not have been born, and therefore it would have been better if Hezekiah's life had not been spared (2 Kings 21:1-9). That is an incorrect inference. We cannot say more than Scripture does nor can we say that Manasseh's wickedness was inevitable. Remember, in any event, that Manasseh repented (2 Chron 33:10-20).

[3]John, in particular, uses the word *sēmeia* (signs) to describe Jesus' miracles.

יְהוָה שָׁלוֹם

Yahweh Shalom

11

The LORD is Peace

On 30th September 1938, Neville Chamberlain, then the prime minister of Great Britain, made a speech from Number 10 Downing Street. For some time he had followed a policy of appeasement toward Hitler and Mussolini. Chamberlain had just returned from a meeting with Hitler in Munich. He described his diplomatic victory with characteristic modesty:

> This is the second time in our history that there has come back from Germany to Downing Street peace with honour. I believe it is peace for our time.

With his usual candour, Winston Churchill described Chamberlain's European escapade as "a total, unmitigated defeat." Soon Britain was at war and, not long after, Chamberlain was out of office. Unfortunately, in this fallen world of ours, lasting peace seems elusive. Is there a simple reason for this elusiveness?

Passage and References

Passage   **Judg. 6:11-24**

References
      Num. 6:22-27; Jer. 6:14; 8;11; Matt. 5:9; 10:34-39;
John 14:25- 27; 20:19-23; Rom. 12:8; 16:20; Gal. 5:22; **Eph. 2:14-18;**
Phil. 4:4-9; 2 Thess. 3:16; Heb. 13:20-21.

Questions

1. Do you think the world is any closer to peace today than it was in the past since we are less bloodthirsty and more civilized? If not, to what do you attribute the problem?

2. Why did Gideon call the altar he erected *Yahweh Shalom*?

3. Appeasement is one way to achieve "peace." How was this working out for the Israelites in relation to Midianite oppression?

4. Apparently the only way to peace for Israel at this time was via conflict? Is this always the case? What about "the soft answer that turns away wrath?" (Prov 15:1)

5. The Hebrew word *shalom* conveys far more than an absence of hostility, an uneasy truce or a subjective sense of tranquillity. Think of some of the synonyms that one could use to convey the holistic idea of "peace."

6. God is described as "the God of peace" (2 Thess 3:16; Heb 13:12- 13). What was the price of peace and reconciliation (Eph 2:14-18)?

7. What did Jesus mean when he said, "Don't think that I have come to bring peace on the earth" (Matt 10:34)?

8. Why should it be "the God of peace" who crushes Satan (Rom 16:20)?

9. Paraphrase the terms, (1) "the peace of God," and (2) "the God of peace" in Phil 4:7, 9).

10. What does Paul mean when he says, "If it is possible, as far as depends on you, live at peace with everyone?" (Rom. 12:18).

Suppose someone in your strata is being really inconsiderate. It may not be wrong to confront the person. But what factors should influence your decision and the manner in which you raise the issue?

Comment

If you visit Israel today, you will notice that the word *Shalom* is used repeatedly. It means more than "peace" in the narrow sense. In Scripture it connotes, among other things, completeness, wholeness, well-being, and even perfection. It is more than the absence of hostility or a sense of tranquillity. Kenneth Hemphill considers some of the passages in which the term is used (Gen 15:16—"full measure"; 1 Kings 8:61—"fully committed"; 9:25—"fulfilled"; 1 Chron 29:19—"wholehearted"; and let's not forget the Aaronic blessing in Num 6:22-27). He then makes this observation:

> The fundamental idea behind the word *shalom* is wholeness in one's relationship with God. *Shalom* defined a harmony of relationship based upon the completion of a transaction, the giving of satisfaction. It does not mean that we simply have a truce, where outward conflict disappears but inner turmoil remains. It is not merely an uneasy cease-fire! In that sense it is appropriate that *shalom* is translated 170 times in our English Bible as *peace*.

Shalom expresses the deepest need and desire of the human heart. In our experience it means a sense of contentment, a freedom from guilt and a satisfaction with life itself.[1]

The human condition is such that a cheap peace is no peace at all. Real peace involves the righting of wrongs. Lasting peace is only possible where justice exists. Genuine peace must contend with the fundamentals of our condition. Such peace, as we shall see, is extremely costly.

In examining the name *Yahweh Shalom,* we are considering an aspect of God's nature that speaks right into one of the greatest needs of humankind. It is true that we encounter the name *Yahweh Shalom* in this form in only one place, and then it is, strictly speaking, the name given to an altar rather than to the LORD. But, as we shall see, God repeatedly reveals himself as the God of peace. It is best to approach the subject by first examining the passage in which the name *Yahweh Shalom* is used and then placing it within the wider context of Scripture.

Gideon's Call
When the Israelites entered the land of Canaan, God promised to bless them abundantly. If, however, they disobeyed him, they were destined to suffer at the hands of their enemies. And it is abundantly clear from the first three chapters of the Book of Judges that they did disobey him. In consequence, they had to face stout resistance from within their borders and devastating incursions from without. The situation was dreadful. For seven years the Midianites, together with the Amalekites and other Eastern peoples, oppressed them. They would wait for the Israelites to plant their crops and then come in their hoards and ruin the crops. There were so many of them and they were so destructive that the Midianite army resembled a swarm of locusts. They did not spare a living thing, neither sheep, nor cattle, nor donkeys. They ravished the land and impoverished the Israelites.

But the Israelites found a way to keep the peace. They prepared shelters for themselves in the mountain clefts, caves and strongholds. When the Midianites invaded the land, the Israelites went into hiding. This would go on year after year until the Israelites were so impoverished that they cried out to the LORD in desperation. Like the rest of his compatriots, young Gideon was taking the course of least resistance. He was threshing wheat in a winepress to keep it from the Midianites. One day a Stranger came and sat down under a nearby oak tree which belonged to Joash, Gideon's father. He greeted Gideon with the words, "The LORD is with you, mighty warrior." Gideon objected. "Sir," he said, "if the LORD is with us, why has all this happened to us?" But the Stranger replied, "Go in the strength you have and save Israel out of Midian's hand. Am I not sending you?" "But Lord," Gideon asked, "how can I save Israel? My clan is the weakest in Manasseh, and I am the least in my family." The LORD answered, "I will be with you, and you will strike down all the Midianites together."

By this time Gideon must have wondered just who it was that was speaking to him. He addressed the Stranger as *Adonai,* which can mean "Lord" or just "Sir." The Stranger's instruction seemed so authoritative. But the ever-cautious Gideon did not want to jump to conclusions. So he asked the Stranger to wait while he prepared a meal. Showing such hospitality to visitors was customary courtesy in the east. But, interestingly, the word used by Gideon to describe the meal was a word that can be used to describe a "meat offering". What Gideon prepared might equally be a meal for a man or an offering to God. We know from Gideon's subsequent request for a sign regarding the fleece (Jud 6:36-40), that he sought to confirm impressions or instructions by asking for a "sign". He was not sure of the identity of the Stranger. If the Stranger treated the offering as a normal meal then he was an ordinary visitor. If he accepted it as an offering, then something extraordinary was happening.

So Gideon prepared the meal and brought it out to the Stranger under the oak tree. The Stranger asked him to place the food on the rock and to pour out the broth. Then with the tip of the staff that was in his hand, the Stranger touched the meat and the unleavened bread. Fire flared from the rock, consuming the meat and the bread. And, in an instant, the Stranger disappeared.

Gideon realized that it was "the angel of the LORD". He cried out, "Ah Sovereign LORD *(Adonai Yahweh)*! I have seen the Angel of the LORD face to face!" Realizing that he had been conversing with God, he expected to die (cf. Ex. 33:20). Immediately the LORD reassured him: "Peace *(Shalom)!* Do not be afraid. You are not going to die." As we examine the passage, and particularly the names used to describe Gideon's visitor, it is clear that this was a "theophany", an appearance of the Lord in angelic form. When we read of "the Angel of the LORD" the reference is not just to one angel among many; it is not even to a special angelic messenger. This is God assuming angelic appearance long before he took on our humanity in the incarnation. The same person is described here as, "the angel of the LORD *(Yahweh)*", "LORD *(Yahweh)*", "Lord *(Adonai)*", "the angel of God *(Elohim)*" and "Sovereign LORD *(Adonai Yahweh)*".

The Name and its Significance
In response to all that had happened, Gideon built an altar to the LORD and called it *Yahweh Shalom*—"The LORD is Peace". This was no doubt because of the LORD's first word to him after he discovered that he had seen the Angel of the LORD—"Peace!" Realizing that God had graciously spared his life, Gideon wished to commemorate the revelation that the LORD is *Yahweh Shalom,* the God of Peace. But there is more to the use of this name than the fact that Gideon's life was spared. The one who revealed himself as *Yahweh Shalom* was about to deliver the Israelites from Midianite oppression.

The Israelites may have thought that their evasive action was affording them a measure of peace. But they had settled for a "peace" with disgrace, a "peace" that, in the long run, cost them so dearly that almost anything was preferable to their enslavement. Now *Yahweh Shalom* is about to give them "peace with honour".

The route to this peace was not going to be easy. In this fallen world it never is. First there has to be trouble. Gideon must risk his life. He must tear down his own father's altar to Baal and cut down the Asherah pole beside it. He must then build an altar to the LORD and sacrifice a mature bull from his father's herd on it, using the wood of the Asherah pole as firewood for the burnt offering. With the help of ten of his servants Gideon waited for nightfall and did as the LORD had commanded him. The next morning the town woke up to find, to its horror, that Baal's altar had been demolished, the Asherah pole cut down and a bull sacrificed on the newly built altar. They were so incensed that they wanted to kill the culprit. Gideon's father came to his son's defence and Gideon was nicknamed "Jerub-Baal", meaning "Let Baal contend". In other words, it was accepted that Gideon had antagonized not just his fellow citizens but Baal himself and had incurred the wrath of the Canaanite god.

The story of Gideon is well known from this point on. When next the Midianites and their allies crossed over the Jordan River to devastate the land, the Spirit of the LORD came upon Gideon and he blew a trumpet, summoning the members of his clan to follow him. Messengers were sent throughout the tribe of Manasseh, calling them to arms. Three of the other northern tribes were also summoned (Asher, Zebulun and Naphtali).

Once again, Gideon sought confirmation, this time by means of his fleece. Then came the troop reductions. First of all 22 000 were allowed to leave because they were terrified. Only 10 000 remained. But another test was required, a test which only 300 passed. It needed to be abundantly clear that God had given the Israelites victory so that they would not arrogate to themselves the credit for the conquest. It was a remarkable victory indeed. *Yahweh Shalom--The LORD is Peace* had restored peace to his people. It was a peace that came not through appeasement but through confrontation.

The God of Peace

Although this is the only time in the Old Testament where God is referred to as *Yahweh Shalom,* the experience of peace is associated with the reign of God in such a way as to make this name implicit in many passages. So, for example, we read in Psalm 29: 11, "The LORD gives strength to his people; the LORD blesses his people with peace." The Good News of peace is the news that God reigns (Isa. 52:7).

The prophets looked forward to a time of unprecedented peace. Time and again, even after the most devastating prophecies of judgment, they envisaged the dawn of universal peace. Naturally Israel is at the centre of the prophecies but their descriptions go much further than a golden age for Israel (Isa. 65:17-25; 66:12; Hos. 14:6-7; Hag. 2:9; Zech. 14:16-17).

In the New Testament God is often referred to as *"the God of Peace".* The language used there is, of course, Greek but the Hebrew equivalent is *Yahweh Shalom* or *Elohim Shalom.* So, for example, Paul says to the Romans: "The God of Peace be with you all" (Rom. 15:33). He refers to God as "the God of peace" in his letters to the Corinthians, the Philippians and the Thessalonians (2 Cor. 13:11; Phil. 4:9; I Thess. 5:23; 2 Thess. 3: 16). This designation is also used by the Writer to the Hebrews (Heb. 13:20).

The Perspective of Scripture

To place this matter of peace in perspective, we need to go right back to the point at which our peace was shattered. The picture painted for us in Genesis 1 and 2 is one of well-being and tranquillity. But with the Fall, strife and disharmony entered. Adam feels ashamed and hides. When God asks him what he has done, he blames Eve and has the audacity to imply that God was partly to blame for his disobedience: "The woman you put here with me - she gave me some fruit from the tree and I ate it" (Gen. 3:12).

Look at the immediate results of human transgression. Mankind is ill-at-ease in God's presence. Adam and Eve start doing stupid things in relation to God, like assuming that he could hide from the all-seeing One. The first marital row takes place. In the very next chapter we see how the disharmony introduced at the fall results in murder as Cain rises up and kills his own brother.

Not until we come to the end of Scripture do we see universal harmony. The picture we are given in the last two chapters of the Bible is one of perfect peace. No war, no hostility, no tension, no murderers or rapists, no idolaters, no liars, no fortune-tellers, nothing impure; only joy and harmony, abundance and the unhindered enjoyment of one another's company. Peace at last!

The Prince of Peace
In between these two events the subject is developed. There is the wonderful prophecy in Isaiah 9:5-7. We are so familiar with the words of verse 6, that we tend to forget that universal peace is tied to the one described as *Sar Shalom* (the Prince of Peace):

> Of the increase of his government
> and peace there will be no end.
> He will reign on David's throne
> and over his kingdom,
> establishing and upholding it

with righteousness and justice
from that time on and for ever.
The zeal of the LORD Almighty
will accomplish this (Isa. 9:5-7).

We can't miss the relationship in this messianic passage between the government of God through the Son he has chosen and the advent of peace. How appropriate it is that from the beginning to the end of Jesus' ministry, the concept of "peace" occupied such an important place. When Jesus was born the angel announced, "Glory to God in the highest and on earth peace to those on whom his favour rests" (Luke 2:14). We hear him telling people whom he healed, "Go in peace" (Luke 7:50; 8:48). We see him rebuking the wind and saying: "Peace be still!" And there was a great calm (Mark 4:30). To his disciples he says, "Peace I leave with you; my peace I give to you. I do not give to you as the world gives. Do not let your hearts be troubled and do not be afraid" (John 14:27). The first words he spoke to his disciples when he appeared to them after his resurrection were: "Peace be with you" (Luke 24:36).

But, interestingly, Jesus said to his disciples: "Do not suppose I have come to bring peace on earth. I did not come to bring peace but a sword" (Matt. 10:34). He explained that, in the process of bringing peace to this wayward world, there would be division and persecution, pain and strife.

A comparison of three verses helps us to see what is happening. In the first God pronounces judgment on "the Serpent". This has been seen by commentators as the first indication in Scripture that God would deal with the problem of sin and rebellion in the universe by means of a member of the human race: "I will put enmity between you and the woman, and between your offspring and hers; he will crush your head and you will strike his heel" (Gen. 3: 15). One of

Eve's descendants would enter into combat with the Serpent. The Serpent would attack him but he would overcome the Serpent.

At the end of Scripture we read of the final judgment: "He (the angel) seized the dragon, that ancient serpent, who is the devil, or Satan, and bound him for a thousand years. . . ." (Rev. 20:2-3). Subsequently he was thrown into the lake of burning sulphur where he is confined for ever (Rev. 20: 10).

There is a little verse at the end of Romans that we usually miss: "The God of peace will soon crush Satan *under your feet*" (Rom. 16:20; italics added). I wonder if Paul was thinking of Genesis 3: 15 when he wrote this sentence. There is no question that Jesus "must reign till he has put all enemies *under his feet*" (I Cor. 15:25; italics added). What is interesting is that we share with him in this great victory. We see this clearly in passages found in Daniel 7, Ephesians 1 and Hebrews 2. In Daniel 7, for example, we notice that the Son of Man "was given authority, glory and sovereign power; all people, nations and men of every language worshipped him. His dominion is an everlasting dominion that will not pass away, and his kingdom is one that will never be destroyed" (Dan. 7: 14). Then we read, "The sovereignty, power and greatness of the kingdoms under the whole heaven will be handed over *to the saints, the people of the Most High.* His kingdom will be an everlasting kingdom and all rulers will worship and obey him" (Dan. 7:27; italics added).

There is such consistency in Scripture. Paul has exactly the same thought: God has raised Christ and seated him at his right hand "far above all rule and authority, power and dominion, and every title that can be given, not only in the present age but also in the one to come. And God placed all things *under his feet* and appointed him to be head over everything *for the church,* which is his body, the fullness of him who fills everything in every way" (Eph. 1:20-23; italics added). The Writer to the Hebrews refers to Psalm 8 in which we are told that God has crowned mankind with glory and honour and put everything *under his feet* (Heb. 2:6-8; italics added). He observes that nothing is excluded from his dominion but that "at present we do not see everything subject to him. But we see Jesus, who was made a little lower than the angels, now crowned with glory and honour because he suffered death. . . ." (cf. Phil. 2:5-11). Here the relationship between the exalted Lord and "his brothers" is stressed: "In bringing many sons to glory, it was fitting that God, for whom and through whom everything exists, should make the author of their salvation perfect through suffering" (Heb. 2:10, cf. Matt. 19:28-30; Luke 19:17; 22: 28-30; Rom. 8:17-21; I Cor. 6:2-3; 2 Tim. 2:11-13).

Implications
First, **there is only one way to a complete and lasting peace**: *Yahweh Shalom*—the LORD is Peace. There is peace in the New Jerusalem because "the dwelling of God is with men, and he will live with them. They will be his people and God himself will be with them and be their God" (Rev. 21:3). Without God there can be no genuine, lasting peace.

Second, **the road to peace is often a road of conflict and strife**. Jesus said, "Blessed are the peacemakers," not, "Blessed are the peace lovers." Sometimes we have to be "troublesome peacemakers". Think of Gideon after he had met with *Yahweh Shalom*. For him the policy of appeasement came to an abrupt end; he had to risk his life. And taking on the Midianites was going to be dangerous in the extreme. The fact is that peace lovers, peace-at-any-price people, bear a measure of responsibility for impropriety and wrongdoing in the world. There is a better example than Gideon. The Prince of Peace himself was often at the centre of controversy. To do good is to oppose evil and to oppose evil is to court the disfavour of those perpetrating it.

Third, **we are recipients of his peace here and now**. The first and most important benefit that comes to us is our reconciliation to God: "Therefore, since we have been justified through faith, we have peace with God through our Lord Jesus Christ" (Rom. 5:1). No need, like Adam, to hide among the bushes. Our sin has been forgiven and our guilt taken away. What's more, "if, when we were God's enemies, we were reconciled to him through the death of his Son, how much more, having been reconciled, shall we be saved through his life? Not only is this so, but we rejoice in God through our Lord Jesus Christ, through whom we have now received reconciliation" (Rom. 5: 10-11).

Fourth, **another important blessing that comes to us is the "miracle" of harmony**. The division between Jew and Gentile went deeper than dislike. There was segregation. But Paul was able to address Jewish and Gentile Christians as members of one body. He attributed their remarkable unity entirely to the work of Jesus: "He himself is our peace, who has made the two one and destroyed the barrier, the dividing wall of hostility. . . . His purpose was to create in himself one new man out of the two, thus making peace. . . . He came and preached peace to you who were far away and peace to those who were near. For through him we both have access to the Father by one Spirit" (Eph 2: 14-18). One of the most compelling effects of the gospel is its ability to engender harmony and peace among the most diverse group of people. Wherever the church follows her Lord, there is a harmony that is supernatural.

Fifth, **there is also the sense of *shalom*, of well-being and serenity, that comes to our hearts and minds**. The peace described in Scripture is relational. It is a harmony between two or more parties. But by his presence in our lives, *Yahweh Shalom* also imparts a sense of peace. Paul encourages us to present our requests to God, with thanksgiving, and assures us that "the peace of God, which transcends understanding, will guard our hearts and minds in Christ Jesus" (Phil 4:7, 9). How God loves it when we come to him, tell him what is troubling us, thank him for his goodness, and trust him to bestow his peace. It is a peace that transcends understanding. Sometimes it seems to descend as a gentle blanket. At other times it appears to emanate from within. We live in the interim between the "already" and the "not yet". God has already given us his Spirit: "The fruit of the Spirit is love, joy, *peace. . . .*" (Gal. 5:22; italics added).

Sixth, **we are to be agents of God's peace in a world characterized by disharmony**. Having reconciled us to himself and created harmony between us and Christians of different backgrounds, God instructs us to be peaceable toward everybody. Jesus said, "Blessed are the peacemakers, for they will be called sons of God" (Mat.t 5:9). Paul made it clear that there would be tension on account of the stand we take but he stressed that any hostility ought not to be on account of belligerence on our part: "If it is possible, as far as depends on you, live at peace with everyone" (Rom. 12:18; cf. I Pet.3:13-17; 4:12-16). As children of *Yahweh Shalom,* we ought to be an anticipation and a sign of the peace that will one day be universal.

In A Nutshell

Summary
"Peace" is one of the key concepts in the Bible. Because of sin and our estrangement from God, peace and harmony between individuals and nations is elusive. God reveals himself to Gideon. When he realizes he has "seen" the LORD, he fears for his life, but God speaks peace to him and he builds an altar to *Yahweh Shalom*.

In *this* instance, the only way to "peace" was conflict. More importantly, the way to permanent peace was extremely costly, but God established peace through the cross and this peace has both vertical and horizontal dimensions. Peace is primarily relational (an objective state of affairs) but it also has an important subjective dimension (a state of heart and mind). The name *Yahweh Shalom* sums up God's great plan of salvation.

A Prayer

We can hardly do better than to pray from our hearts the prayer attributed to St. Francis of Assisi:

Lord, make me an instrument of you peace!
Where there is hatred let me sow love;
where there is injury, pardon; where there is doubt, faith;
where there is despair, hope; where there is darkness, light;
where there is sadness, joy.

"Now may the Lord of peace (Greek: *Kurios tēs eirēnēs*; Hebrew: *Yahweh Shalom*) himself give you peace at all times and in every way. The Lord be with you" (2 Thess 3:16).

NOTE

[1] Kenneth Hemphill, *The Names of God* (Nashville, TN: Broadman and Holman Publishers, 2001), 144.

יְהוָה צְבָאוֹת

Yahweh Tsava'ōth

12

The LORD Almighty

In the King James Version, *Yahweh Tsava'ōth* is rendered "The LORD of Hosts." The translators of the NIV preferred "The LORD Almighty," believing no doubt that it conveyed the sense of the name better. We need, of course, to remember that everything that is conveyed by the name *Yahweh* holds good for each of the compound names of the LORD. As *Yahweh*, he is the self-existent God who is always true to his nature and faithful to his covenant. But, as we have seen, suffixes are added to highlight a particular attribute of God or a dimension of his interaction with us.

Passage and References

Passage: 1 Sam. 17:31-54.

References
     Gen. 32:1-2; Josh. 5:13-14 ("the army of the LORD--*tsavā' Yahweh*"); Psa. 24:10; **Isa. 6:1-7**; 44:6-8; **Hag. 2:1-9**; **Zech. 4:6-8**; Mal. 3:6-12.

Questions

1.   Having read the passage and looked up the references, what is your initial understanding of the name *Yahweh Tsava'ōth*? If you had to choose between the KJV translation, "the LORD of Hosts," and the

NIV translation, "the LORD Almighty," which would you choose and why?

2. **1 SAM. 17:31-54.** What made David so convinced that he would succeed against Goliath?

3. Why did he make specific reference to *Yahweh Tsava'ōth* when he told Goliath that God would grant him victory?

4. **ISA. 6:1-7.** Isaiah saw a vision of the Lord (*Adonai*) but heard the seraphim extolling *Yahweh Tsava'ōth* whose glory filled the earth. Do you see any significance in the reference to God as *Yahweh Tsava'ōth* in this passage? Could Isaiah's state of mind (Uzziah's death) have been a reason why it was good for him to hear this name on the lips of the seraphim?

5. **HAG. 2:1-9.** Why was there such repetition on the name *Yahweh Tsava'ōth* in the Lord's word to the disheartened builders of the second temple?

6.   What in this message contributes to our understanding of the meaning of the name *Yahweh Tsava'ōth*?

7.   **ZECH. 4:6.** Zechariah saw a *menorah* but it differed in several respects from the one that would have been in the temple, most notably that it had a never-ending supply of oil. How does this picture lead to the statement, "'Not by might nor by power but by my Spirit,' says *Yahweh Tsava'ōth*"?

8.   What is the essential message of this statement and what does it tell us about the role of *Yahweh Tsava'ōth* in our Christian service?

9.   Can you think of any situation (past, current, or future) in which you needed or need to be particularly aware that God is *Yahweh Tsava'ōth*?

10. How might you strengthen your faith so that when you face a Goliath, your instinctive reaction is to see God as *Yahweh Tsava'ōth*, thereby putting the problem or obstacle into correct perspective?

Comment

The Hebrew word *tsavā'* means a host (an army). *Tsava'ōth* is the plural of *tsavā'*, hence the title "the LORD of Hosts." More often than not, the term *tsava'ōth* refers to the armies of Israel. If that's all there was to it, we might be tempted to think that the name simply identifies God as the God who was with Israel in battle. But that would be to limit the richness contained in the name to which Scripture refers so often (well over 200 times) and in such different contexts. Yes it is true that at the end of a period of 430 years, to the very day, "all *Yahweh's* hosts (*tsava'ōth*) left Egypt" (Exod 12:41). But the term *tsava'ōth* is sometimes used to refer to angels (Psa 103:20-21; 148:2). So, clearly, more is intended by the use of this name than that God is head of the armies of Israel.

The best way to determine the meaning of a compound name is by a careful study of its usage throughout Scripture. An interesting and enriching picture emerges. We shall focus briefly on four passages in chronological order; the inferences drawn from these passages are consistent with the many references to *Yahweh Tsava'ōth* in the Bible.

David's Perspective

Think for a moment of the *tsavā'* of Israel quivering in its boots as Goliath marched up and down taunting the Israelite soldiers. David's instinctive reaction indicates a faith in God that was simple; that he took God at his word and found the Philistine's taunts scandalous. Eventually young David went out to meet the giant. Goliath was insulted when he saw that David was just a boy and that he had come out with a staff and a sling: "Am I a dog that you come out to me with sticks?" And the Philistine cursed David by his gods. . . ." David's response went right to the heart of the matter: "You come against me with a sword and spear and javelin, but I come against you in the name of *Yahweh Tsava'ōth*, the God of the armies of Israel, whom you have defied. This day *Yahweh* will hand you over to me" (1 Sam. 17:43-46). In David's mind Goliath didn't have a hope; he had dared to defy *Yahweh Tsava'ōth*. He was convinced that *Yahweh Tsava'ōth* was in ultimate control of all things. As far as he was concerned, it was not he but Goliath who was being audacious.

Isaiah's Vision

It's amazing what we are able to see once we have a clue regarding the meaning of these names of God. Think once more of the well-known passage in Isaiah 6:

In the year that King Uzziah died, I saw the Lord (*Adonai*) seated on a throne, high and exalted, and the train of his robe filled the temple. Above him were the seraphs. . . . And they were calling to one another, "Holy, holy, holy is *Yahweh Tsava'ōth*; the whole earth is full of his glory. . . ."

"Woe is me!" I cried. "I am ruined! For I am a man of unclean lips and I live among a people of unclean lips, and my eyes have seen the King, *Yahweh Tsava'ōth*" (Isa. 6:1-4).

As Isaiah heard the seraphim cry, "Holy, holy, holy is *Yahweh Ts'vaoth*, the whole earth is full of his glory," he feared for his life. He had "seen" *Yahweh Ts'vaoth*, the exalted one, the real King seated upon the throne of the universe. We are certainly shown something of God's majesty but we also realize, in view of the context, that he is being portrayed as being in absolute control over all things; indeed the whole earth is full of his glory.

Haggai's Word
The three post-exilic prophets (Haggai, Zechariah, and Malachi) lay emphasis on the fact that God is *Yahweh Tsava'ōth*. The name occurs no fewer than 86 times in 19 chapters! When God's people returned from exile, they really did put first things first. Not only did they forego relative ease in Babylonia, but they also gave freewill offerings towards the rebuilding of the house of God and began the work as soon as they possibly could. But, as a result of sustained opposition on the part of the surrounding people, they downed tools and for fifteen years not another stone was laid. Meanwhile they worked on their own homes. The opposition waned but things just didn't work out for them. God raised up two prophets, Haggai and Zechariah, who challenged the people to recommence the building of the temple. The leaders and all the people heeded the message and got to work.

After a month God spoke to them again. Possibly they were losing heart. The dating of the prophecy was important (Lev. 23:33; Hag. 2:1). The Feast of Tabernacles was a time when, among other things, the harvest was celebrated (Lev. 23:39-43). But, although they were obeying God, their harvest was meager and there was so much to do. The foundations did not look too impressive. The opposition had not gone away; if anything it had been rekindled by their renewed efforts. With the meaning of the name in mind, notice the repetition of *Yahweh Tsava'ōth* in Haggai's message:

This is what *Yahweh Tsava'ōth* says: "In a little while I will once again shake the heavens and the earth, the sea and the dry land. I will shake all nations, and the desired of all nations will come, and I will fill this house with glory," says *Yahweh Tsava'ōth*. "The silver is mine and the gold is mine," declares *Yahweh Tsava'ōth*. "The glory of the present house will be greater than the glory of the former house," says *Yahweh Tsava'ōth*. "And in this place I will grant peace," declares *Yahweh Tsava'ōth* (Hag. 2:6-9).

There is no redundancy here! The repetition of the name is intentional; in fact it is the whole point of the message. God is saying, "I am speaking to you and I am *Yahweh Tsava'ōth*. Everything is at my disposal and everybody is ultimately under my control."

But what actually happened after this prophecy? Believe it or not, matters took a turn for the worse. The building inspector arrived in the person of Tattenai, the governor of the province of Trans-Euphrates. He wanted to know who had authorized the building operation and took down a list of names of the men working on the construction (Ezra 5:3-5). A report was sent to King Darius who ordered that a search be made in the archives at Babylon. It appeared that matters were going from bad to worse. But there they found a copy of the decree of Cyrus (Ezra 6:6-12). And *Yahweh Tsava'ōth* not only afforded them protection, but also provided their needs, courtesy of Darius. They had to do what they could do and God, *Yahweh Tsava'ōth*, undertook to do what only he could do. He is the one who marshals events and circumstances, friends and foes, to serve his purpose. He is the General in overall command.

Zechariah's Perspective

Zechariah was speaking to the same people as Haggai. His ministry was different from that of Haggai in that he would often describe a vision and then declare its message. He saw a solid gold lamp-stand (*menorah*) with an endless supply of oil. It was God's way of assuring the discouraged people that he would enable them to complete what they had started in his name. God gave the prophet a message for the leader, Zerubbabel: "'Not by might, nor by power, but by my Spirit,' says *Yahweh Ts'vaoth*" (Zech. 4:6). God promised to turn what seemed like a mighty mountain into level ground (Zech. 4:7-10). That's what he is able to do because he is *Yahweh Tsava'ōth*.

Jesus and *Yahweh Tsava'ōth*

All that is contained in the name *Yahweh Tsava'ōth* applies fully to the Lord Jesus since he is *Yahweh*, and is co-equal with the Father and the Holy Spirit. Right now he exercises sovereign power (Col. 1:15-17; Heb. 1:3). But as we focus on the life he lived as man, it is clear that he looked upon the Father as *Yahweh Tsava'ōth*, the one who was in total control of everything, whom he could trust completely (e.g. Matt. 5:45; John 11:41; 19:8-11; Matt. 26:52-54).

The Meaning of the Name

What exactly is signified by the name *Yahweh Tsava'ōth*? Commenting on the name, F. B. Meyer said: "[We conceive] of angels and worlds, of the armies of heaven and the elements of matter, of winds and waves, of life and death, as a vast ordered army, obedient to the commands of their Captain, [*Yahweh Tsava'ōth*]." The word "providence" comes to mind. God is able to marshal the forces of nature and even the voluntary acts of people to accomplish his purposes. He is sovereign, he is all-powerful, and he contends for his people. He is the God who "comes through" when the odds are stacked up against us.

No matter how impossible the situation may seem—a Goliath on the horizon, inadequate resources, a complicated family problem—he is able to manage the situation. He employs people, both well-intentioned and antagonistic, and events, both favorable and adverse, in order to accomplish his will. He can do this in your domestic situation, in the church, in the nation, and in the world. He *is* doing it in history. When young David confronted Goliath in the name of *Yahweh Tsava'ōth*, he was speaking in the name of the one who created gravity and the atmosphere, the laws of aero-dynamics and the human body with its points of vulnerability, the one who had watched over the sheep in his care and helped him to develop his ability to use a sling. As *Yahweh Tsava'ōth* he could marshal these elements to fulfill his purpose. He could also touch the heart of a heathen king and turn the antipathy of the enemies of Israel to great advantage. He is *Yahweh Tsava'ōth*, the faithful God who commits himself to us and who marshals all events and resources to his glory. He is deserving of our trust.

Some years ago, I was involved in the organization of a mission at which Franklin Graham was the evangelist. It was a huge undertaking with many facets, the assembly of a committee, the rental of numerous venues including a large soccer stadium, transport arrangements and a massive budget. As the time approached, we had to contend with a number of obstacles. In one particular executive meeting, the magnitude of the undertaking struck us and one could feel the consternation in the room. Then one committee member, sensing our trepidation, smiled calmly and remarked, "God is in big trouble now!" There was a pause and we saw the absurdity of our misgivings. We laughed at the short-sightedness of our own lack of faith. What seemed so daunting to us was no problem to *Yahweh Tsava'ōth*!

In A Nutshell

Summary

The name *Yahweh Tsava'ōth* occurs frequently in Scripture. It depicts God as the one who is in ultimate control of all things, animate and inanimate. He is able to marshal angels and worlds, the armies of heaven and the elements of matter, winds and waves, life and death, as a vast ordered army, obedient to the commands of their Captain.

That is what is implied when David faces Goliath in the name of *Yahweh Tsava'ōth*. The seraphim worship *Yahweh Tsava'ōth* whose glory fills the earth, and Isaiah sees him as the true King, seated upon the throne of the universe. Through the prophet Haggai, he assures his people that it is he who controls all the resources they could possibly need. Through Zechariah he speaks to his people who face a daunting assignment that it is "'Not by might, nor by power, but by my Spirit,' says *Yahweh Tsava'ōth*."

A Prayer

O LORD, you are the *Yahweh Tsava'ōth*. Help me to remember that you are seated upon the throne of the universe. Forgive me for placing limitations on you in my own thinking. And forgive me for presuming to undertake your work in my own feeble strength.

Remind me that when you open a door no one can shut it, and when you close a door, no one can open it (Rev. 3:7). When I face an impossible situation, help me to see that nothing is impossible for you (Luke 1:37; 18:27). Help me to learn, as David did, to live in fellowship with you as I go about my everyday tasks so that when I face a giant, I do not measure him against me but against you. Help me to see that mountains can be reduced to plains before *Yahweh Tsava'ōth* (Zech. 4:7).

Father, when I pray that your name will be hallowed, that your kingdom will come and that your will be done on earth as it is in heaven, help me to remember that I am praying to the one who is *Yahweh Tsava'ōth* and that nothing is more certain than that this petition will be granted. Even now, may your great name be honoured.

Amen.

יְהוָה רֹעִי
Yahweh Rō'i
13

The LORD, My Shepherd

Not everybody sees *Yahweh Rō'i* as one of the compound names of God. On balance, it certainly adds to the overall picture. The opening words of the 23rd psalm are well known and the Sovereign LORD (*Adonai Yahweh*) declares, "I myself will search for my sheep and look after them. As a shepherd looks after his scattered flock when he is with them, so I will look after my sheep" (Ezek 34:11-12). The Lord Jesus identifies himself as the Good Shepherd (John 10:11, 14, 27-29). So there is more than enough reason to see this designation as revealing a quality that is intrinsic to God's nature.

Passage and References

Passage: **Psa. 23**

References
    2 Sam. 5:2; Isa. 40:10-11; Jer. 31:10-11; **Ezek. 34:11-16, 20- 24, 31**; Zech. 13:7; Matt. 26:31; **John 10:11, 14, 27-30**; 21:15-19; Acts 20:28; Heb. 13:20-21; 1 Pet. 2:21-25; 5:1-4; Rev. 7:15-17.

Questions

1.   React to the comment: "We should jettison the image of the shepherd in our culture and find a more suitable one since most of us

are not really familiar with the imagery associated with a middle-eastern shepherd."

2.   What do you think it is about Psalm 23 that makes it a favorite of so many Christian readers?

3.   **EZEKIEL 34: 1-16, 20-24, 31**. What was it about Israel's shepherds that caused the LORD to dismiss them?

4.   What did the LORD say he would do about it (Ezek. 34:11-16)? How do you feel about his response?

5.   Do you think that the LORD was promising to raise King David from the dead (Ezek. 34:20-24)? If not, what does the promise mean?

6. **PSALM 23.** As you reflect on the lines of Psalm 23, can you see how the shepherd analogy applies to you? What, in particular, do you find encouraging?

7. What, according to this passage are the good things a shepherd does for his sheep? And how does this compare with the shepherds of Ezek. 34?

8. **JOHN 10:1-21, 27-30.** When Jesus described himself as the Good Shepherd, do you think that he was intentionally relating these promises to himself? Think of the extent to which he went for the sake of his sheep. What shepherd qualities do you value most highly?

Comment

It is likely that Psalm 23 was written in the latter years of David's reign as Israel's shepherd-king (2 Sam. 5:2). No doubt he reflected on the days of his youth as a shepherd on the hills surrounding Bethlehem. Herbert Stevenson comments:

He realized that all that he had sought to be to his sheep, and more, the LORD was to him. So he wrote "*Yahweh Rō'i*—The LORD [is] My

Shepherd. . . ." He had cared for his sheep, anticipating their needs and watching over them with kindly concern; he had protected them from danger, even at peril of his life when he slew a lion and a bear; he had led them when necessary to fresh pastures—and though the journey may be arduous and the road rough, he had guided and tended them through all the hazards of the way. In like manner the LORD was with him, caring, leading, providing.[1]

The image of the shepherd is applied to kings and teachers and most importantly, to the LORD himself. Human shepherds sometimes fail and care more for their own interests and reputation than for the sheep, but the divine Shepherd cares for the flock to the extent of laying down his life for the sheep (Ezek. 34:1-6, 11-12; John 10:11, 14-15). Nathan Stone cites Harriet-Louise Patterson's observations about shepherding in Israel in *Around the Mediterranean with My Bible*:

The Palestine shepherd lives night and day with his animals. He establishes a degree of intimacy with them that is touching to observe. He calls them all by their names and they, knowing his voice and hearing his only, heed. He protects the sheep from thieves and preying animals who would devour them at night, by sleeping in the opening of the often makeshift sheepfold and they, sensing his watchfulness, fear "no evil." He provides pasture and water even in the wilderness and the presence of enemies and they, casting all their anxiety upon him, are fed. There is a singular commitment between the shepherd and his sheep which, after one has visited Palestine and observed it, makes the symbol of the good Shepherd peculiarly apt and the Twenty-third Psalm strangely moving.[2]

When the LORD is portrayed as the ultimate Shepherd, both the intimacy of the relationship between the shepherd and the sheep, and the total commitment of the Shepherd to the well-being of the sheep, are in view.

Yahweh Ro'i (Psalm 23)

So much can be said about the 23rd psalm. Several books have been written about it and it is certainly possible to expound the spiritual significance of every line.[3] We can't do that here. All I would suggest is that you put yourself in the position of a sheep (as unappealing as that may be). What would your needs be? What dangers would you face? Could you cope without a shepherd?

Now briefly reflect on each line of the psalm. "I shall not be in want." That's a general statement affirming the psalmist's confidence that the shepherd will supply all his needs. The green pastures and quiet waters certainly paint a picture of tranquility but the primary thought would be of sustenance, the provision of what is necessary for the maintenance of life. The restoration of one's soul can refer to the general refreshment but would be especially relevant after a period of difficulty or waywardness. Guidance is an important part of a shepherd's function. He knows the appropriate paths better than the sheep do. He leads us in the paths of righteousness. But the reality of the terrain is such that access to green pastures and quiet waters is sometimes by way of dangerous mountain passes. At such times, in "the valley of the shadow of death," the vigilance and care of the shepherd are especially needed. The rod and staff come in handy in keeping the sheep from the edge of the precipice. Another psalm comes to mind: "He will not let your foot slip—he who watches over you will not slumber; indeed, he who watches over Israel will neither slumber nor sleep" (Psa. 121:3-4).

"You prepare a table before me in the presence of my enemies." Enemies are present. Wolves and other animals of prey were never too far from a middle-eastern flock. But between them and the sheep was the shepherd. If he was a good shepherd, he would face danger and even death for the sheep (1 Sam. 17:34-37; John 10:11-13). If we have no enemies in this life, we are probably doing something wrong or, at least, we are not doing something right. One could almost write a "Life of David" using the lines of the psalm as chapter headings.

Anointing has a triple meaning here. Sheep were "anointed" to repel insects, to avoid conflicts, and to help heal wounds. David's anointing was as shepherd-king of Israel (2 Sam. 5:2-3), and our anointing is indicative of the presence of the Holy Spirit (2 Cor. 1:21- 22; 1 John 2:27). The upshot of the shepherd's care is a cup of blessing that overflows and the assurance of the permanent presence of the Shepherd. What a wonderful analogy: *Yahweh Ro'i*—the LORD is my Shepherd."

Knowing the Shepherd
Some years ago I read of an occasion when an actor was asked to recite the 23rd psalm at a gathering. His dramatic ability, his resonant voice, and his impeccable diction drew the admiration of those present. Someone in the crowd had heard an elderly country minister preach on the psalm, and the minister happened to be in attendance. He asked if the minister would also recite the psalm. The old vicar was reluctant to do so, but the people were insistent and so he obliged. Something unusual happened. Untrained in speech and drama and with less-than-perfect diction, the old minister recited the psalm right from his heart. The people were deeply moved as the truth contained in each line struck home. Many tears were shed. One of the assembled guests expressed his amazement at the impact. Turning to the person next to him, he asked, "What was the difference?" His neighbour replied, "One thing

is clear: the actor knows the 23rd psalm, but obviously the minister knows the Shepherd!"

Perhaps this is the best thing about the psalm. David was in absolutely no doubt about the power and majesty of *Yahweh*. There is no hint of irreverence. But he speaks of an intimate relationship and his personal care, his guidance and his provision: "*Yahweh Rō'i*— the LORD is *my* Shepherd!"

My Servant David (Ezek. 34:20-24, 31)

The LORD speaks against the shepherds of Israel. Such is their self-centeredness that, in effect, "the flock lacks a shepherd" (Ezek 34:8). But the LORD says, "I myself will search for my sheep and look after them" (Ezek 34:11). God speaks of a day when the ideal shepherd takes care of his flock: "I will place over them one shepherd, my servant David, and he will tend them; he will tend them and be their shepherd. I, *Yahweh*, will be their God and my servant David will be prince among them. I, *Yahweh*, have spoken" (Ezek. 34:24).

David was, of course, long gone when Ezekiel prophesied. The commentary in the Jewish Study Bible reads as follows: "God's rule will be manifested in the establishment of David as ruler. . . . Though other biblical passages imagine a descendant of David as the ideal future king (e.g. Isa. 11:1-10), this passage seems to envisage a return of David himself, the earlier ideal king."[4] Surely this cannot be a reference to a revived David; taken with other references, it seems obvious that the reference is to David's greater son (2 Sam. 7:8, 11- 13, 16; Isa. 9:6-7; Jer. 23:5; 30;9; Ezek. 37:24-25; Hosea 3:5; Matt. 1:1; 12:23; 22:43-45; Luke 1:69; Acts 2:29-34; 2 Tim. 2:8; Rev. 22:16). What an amazing set of prophecies!

The Good Shepherd (John 10:11-18)

The ultimate fulfillment of God's undertaking to shepherd the flock is found in the person of the Good Shepherd. The lines drawn in the Old Testament converge in the One who is the heir to David's throne. During his ministry he saw the crowds and was moved with compassion toward them for they were like sheep without a shepherd (Mark 6:34). At the end of his ministry, when he was arrested his disciples fled in fulfillment of Zechariah's prophecy: "I will smite the shepherd and the sheep will be scattered" (Zech 13:7; Mark 14:27).

In John 10 Jesus emphasizes the most important qualities of a true shepherd in contrast to the self-centeredness of false shepherds. A true shepherd is recognized by the gate-keeper and his voice is known by his sheep. Each sheep is important to him; he knows every one of them by name. He leads them and they follow because they recognize his voice and know they are in safe hands. When they are in the fold, he lies across the entrance ("I am the gate for the sheep") so that they cannot wander off, and no wild animal can get at them without crossing his body. His purpose is to preserve their lives and he wants them to have life in full measure.

Jesus states categorically: "*I am* the good shepherd." He then zeros in on the greatest quality of any shepherd. A hired hand will run for his life in the face of danger, leaving the flock at the mercy of a ravenous wolf or a marauding bear but a devoted shepherd will risk his life for the sake of the sheep. In Jesus' case, he not only risks his life *exposing* himself to injury and possible death; he knowingly lays it down, *surrendering* himself to certain death. So bold and outrageous was this statement that some concluded that he was demon-possessed and raving mad. The significance of Jesus' words is not lost on D. A. Carson:

The shepherd does not die for his sheep to serve as an example, throwing himself off a cliff in a grotesque and futile display while bellowing, "See how much I love you!" No, the assumption is that the sheep are in mortal danger; that in their defense the shepherd loses his life; and that by his death they are saved. That, and that alone, is what makes him *the good shepherd*.[5]

The lengths to which the Good Shepherd will go fill us with certainty. Such is his commitment to his sheep that he can say: "My sheep listen to my voice; I know them and they follow me. I give them eternal life and they shall never perish; no one will snatch them out of my hand. My Father has given them to me and no one is able to snatch them out of my Father's hand. I and the Father are one" (John 10:27-30).

It is little wonder that the image persisted and became the primary way in which ministers of the New Covenant were to see themselves. They serve as under-shepherds, and ought to do so with self-sacrificing commitment , but they always do so in the service of the one who is described as "the Chief Shepherd" and "that great Shepherd of the sheep" (Heb 13:20; 1 Pet 5:4). He has exclusive title to the name *Yahweh Rō'i,* the LORD — my Shepherd.

In A Nutshell

Summary
It is likely that David wrote the 23rd Psalm later in life. He reflected on God's goodness in terms of a faithful shepherd. The metaphor is particularly appropriate in view of the devoted shepherd's care for the sheep. This makes the psalm a masterpiece. But there were also inconsiderate and self-indulgent shepherds in Israel, so God undertakes to care for his own flock. He promises the arrival of one who will be the shepherd *par excellence.* In identifying himself as the Good Shepherd, Jesus lays claim to these prophecies. The LORD himself is our shepherd— *Yahweh Rō'i.* David could describe Yahweh as *Rō'i*—my shepherd, and so can we. Our security is grounded in that great fact: "My sheep listen to my voice; I know them and they follow me. I give them eternal life and they shall never perish; no one can snatch them out of my hand" (John 10:27-28).

A Prayer

Lord, you are the Good Shepherd and you are my Shepherd. You are worthy of my complete confidence. You laid down your life for me. Because of your care, I shall not be in want. You provide me with food for my body and my soul. You guide me into righteousness and you keep me in times of danger. You protect me against those who seek my harm and you even keep me from harming myself.

You are *Yahweh Rō'i—my* Shepherd. I hear your voice and I am secure in the knowledge no one is able to snatch me from your hand. I rejoice in your goodness and believe that "goodness and love will follow me all the days of my life" and I will be with you forever. Thanks be to God for his indescribable gift (2 Cor 9:15).

Amen.

NOTES

[1]Herbert F. Stevenson, *Titles of the Triune God: Studies in Divine Self-Revelation* (London: Marshall, Morgan and Scott, 1955), 81-82.

[2]Nathan Stone, *Names of God* (Chicago, IL: Moody Publishers, 2010 ed. originally published, 1944), 168-69.

[3]For example, F. B Meyer, *The Shepherd Psalm* (Fearn, Scotland: Christian Focus Publications, 2005); Max Lucado, *Safe in the Shepherd's Arms* (Nashville, TN: Thomas Nelson, 2010); Philip Keller, *A Shepherd Looks at Psalm 23* (Grand Rapids, MI: Zondervan, 1970).

[4]Adele Berlin and Marc Zvi Brettler, eds. *The Jewish Study Bible*. Jewish Publication Society: Tanakh Translation (Oxford: Oxford University Press, 2004), 1109.

[5]D. A. Carson, *The Gospel According to John*. The Pillar New Testament Commentary (Grand Rapids: William B. Eerdmans, 1991).

יְהוָה צִדְקֵנוּ
Yahweh Tsidqenu
14

The LORD Our Righteousness

While each of the titles in this series refers to the triune God, Father--Son and Holy Spirit--the particular name we are considering in this study is applied primarily to the Lord Jesus as Israel's Messiah and our Saviour.

Passages and References

Passages: **Isa. 6:9-13; 11:1-5; Jer. 23:5-6; Zech. 6:12-13.**

References

Jer. 33:14-16; **Zech. 3:6-8; Rom. 3:21-24;** 10:1-4; Phil. 3:6-9; 2 Cor. 5:21; 1 Pet. 3:18.

Questions

1. Is it accurate to say that under the dispensation of the law, God gave people an opportunity to achieve righteousness by keeping his commandments, but now, under the new dispensation, righteousness comes by faith? (Gal. 3:21-25; 2 Tim. 1:9-10; 1 Pet. 1:20)

2. If we consider Isa. 6:11-13, would it be right say that God's plan was to concentrate his plan to bring salvation in one place (or person)? (Gal. 3:15-16)

3. To whom do you think Isaiah, Jeremiah and Zechariah were referring when they spoke of the Branch? (Isa. 11:1-5; Jer. 23:5-6; Zech. 3:6-8; 6:12-13)

4. What do you think is meant when the Branch is described as "*Yahweh Tsidqenu*—The LORD our Righteousness"?

5. Although an understanding of the righteousness that comes exclusively by faith in Jesus was only possible once Jesus had died in our place, there are pointers to this truth in the Old Testament. Can you think of some of them? (e.g. Gen. 15:6; Deut. 6:10-12; 9:4-6; the sacrificial system; Psa. 32:1-2).

6. Explain to a person who assumes that salvation is God's response to our good behaviour what you understand by the name *Yahweh Tsidqenu.*

Comment

What we are about to consider gives us an insight into God's saving purpose for the whole of humankind. His "program" of salvation was revealed progressively in history, but it is all part of a single plan. That's why we find so much about it in the Old Testament. Paul explains that the grace we have received through the gospel, "was given us in Christ Jesus before the beginning of time, but it has now been revealed through the appearing of our Saviour, Christ Jesus, who has destroyed death and has brought life and immortality to light through the gospel" (2 Tim. 1 :9-10).

The Prophetic Setting

The passage in which God reveals himself as *Yahweh Tsidkenu* is part of a fascinating stream of messianic prophecy (Jer. 23:5-6). You may well have been puzzled by a term that is used by three of the great Old Testament prophets: Isaiah, Jeremiah and Zechariah. What exactly did they mean when they referred to a person by the odd-sounding title, *the Branch?*

To appreciate what is meant, we need to move systematically through three Old Testament passages and then see how the prophetic statements are fulfilled in God's provision of the gift of righteousness through Jesus. We have already considered the account in Isaiah 6 of the LORD's appearance to Isaiah: "In the year in which King Uzziah died I saw the Lord seated on a throne, high and exalted. . . ." (Isa. 6:1-8). We know that Isaiah said, "Woe to me, I am ruined. . ." We know that the Lord asked him, "Whom shall I send and who will go for us?" and that Isaiah answered, "Here am I, send me." Usually that's where we leave the chapter.

The Stump of Jesse

But the rest of the passage is extremely significant. The Lord made it clear that Isaiah's ministry was not going to seem very successful. In fact, the people were going to disobey and their hearts would be calloused, rendering judgment inevitable. Isaiah's ministry, in other words, was to precipitate God's judgment (Isa 6:9-13). Then, when the cities lay in ruins and the people were in captivity, God would, in a sense, make a fresh beginning: "As the terebinth and oak leave stumps when they are cut down, so the holy seed will be the stump in the land" (Isa. 6:13).

The Branch

This is how God worked. He narrowed things down. In order to reach the world, he chose one nation, then one tribe in the nation, then a family and ultimately one person from that family. It may have seemed that his purpose was defeated when the tree was felled, but the stump remained and we see God's plan beginning to unfold.

> A shoot will come up
> from the stump of Jesse (David's father),
> From his roots *a Branch* will bear fruit.
> The Spirit of the LORD will rest on him-
> the Spirit of wisdom and of understanding,
> the Spirit of counsel and of power,
> the Spirit of knowledge and of the fear of the LORD. . . .
> Righteousness will be his belt
> and faithfulness the sash around his waist
> (Isa. 11:1-2, 5; emphasis added).

So Isaiah anticipates that when the "tree" of Israel has been cut back, and all that is left is a stump, a shoot will come up. From Isaiah's description, the Branch is obviously a person. But who is he? In Jeremiah, we again read about *the Branch*. But Jeremiah tells us something more: he will be called *"Yahweh Tsidkenu*—The LORD our Righteousness."

> "The days are coming,"
> declares the LORD,
> "when I will raise up to David
> *a righteous Branch,*
> a King who will reign wisely
> and do what is just and right in the land.
> In his days Judah will be saved
> and Israel will live in safety.
> This is the name by which he will be called:
> *Yahweh Tsidkenu*--The LORD Our Righteousness
> (Jer. 23:5-6; emphasis added).

There is a similar prophecy in Jeremiah 33:14-16. The picture is developed further in the prophecies of Zechariah. When the Jewish exiles returned to their homeland under Zerubbabel they were accompanied by a High Priest by the name of Joshua. As the spiritual leader of the people he occupied an important position alongside the civic leader, Zerubbabel (Hag. 1: 1, 12, 14; 2:2; Zech. 3: 1-10). God told him that he and his associates were men symbolic of things to come and added: "I am going to bring my servant, *the Branch*" (Zech. 3:8; emphasis added).

In Zechariah 6 we are given an amazing insight. In the Old Testament, the offices of king and priest could never be combined. Kings had to come from the tribe of Judah and the family of David, and priests from the tribe of Levi and the family of Aaron. Not even the Levites, who performed special temple duties, were allowed to usurp the role of priest (Num. 16:1-50; Heb. 5:4). With this in mind, God's instruction to Zechariah to take silver and gold and to make a crown and to set it upon the head of Joshua, the High Priest, must have seemed strange, to say the least. He was to tell Joshua,

> This is what the LORD Almighty says, "Here is the man whose name is *the Branch,* and he will branch out from this place and build the temple of the LORD . . . and he will be clothed with majesty and will sit and rule on his throne. And he will be a priest on his throne" (Zech. 6:12-13; emphasis added).

The Israelites knew that it was simply not possible for any man to be "a priest on his throne." They would have understood that this was a picture, that Joshua's coronation was indeed "symbolic of things to come." Only with the wisdom of hindsight do we understand how Jesus could be a priest *par excellence* by virtue of his qualifications and the atoning sacrifice he made. When we read the Book of Hebrews (chapter 7 in particular), we understand how it was possible for one person to be both a King and a Priest. And yet, contrary to the Old Testament order, even here in Zechariah we are told that the one whose name is "the Branch" would be a royal priest. It is amazing how one passage of Scripture sheds light upon another. There can be no doubt that Psalm 110, which refers to David in the first place, is a messianic psalm (cf. Matt. 22:41-46; I Cor. 15:25). In this psalm there is a reference that only makes sense when we are able to see it in the light of the teaching of the Book of Hebrews:

> The LORD has sworn
> and will not change his mind:
> "You are a priest for ever,
> in the order of Melchizedek" (Psa. 110:4).

Zechariah portrays the "Branch" as "a priest on his throne" and the Writer to the Hebrews explains how someone from the tribe of Judah and the family of David could exercise a high-priestly ministry.

What we have said is even more clear if another priest like Melchizedek appears, one who has become a priest not on the basis of a regulation as to his ancestry but on the basis of the power of an indestructible life. . . . Unlike the other high priests, he does not need to offer sacrifices day after day, first for his own sins, and then for the sins of the people. He sacrificed for their sins once for all when he offered himself. For the law appoints as high priests men who are weak; but the oath, which came after the law, appointed the Son, who has been made perfect for ever (Heb. 7:15, 27-28).

When we encounter the term *Yahweh Tsidkenu*--The LORD Our Righteousness--it is in the context of messianic prophecy. It is the Messiah who is called *Yahweh Tsidqenu.*

God's single plan
God has a single plan of salvation and it all revolves around the concept of RIGHTEOUSNESS. Righteousness is a comprehensive concept. It can be used to denote a person who is good, dependable and fair. The righteous are those who live life God's way. Often "the righteous" are contrasted with "the wicked" (Psa. 1:6; 37:16; Prov. 10:11; Jer. 12:1; Hab. 1:13; Mal. 3:18; Matt. 9:13; Rom. 5:7). There are four simple but important things that we can say about this righteousness as it is presented to us in Scripture.

1. **Righteousness is what God is**. The Psalmist tells us: "The LORD is righteous in all his ways" (Psa 145:17); "Your righteousness is everlasting" (Psa. 119:142).

2. **Righteousness is what we are not!** The Writer of Ecclesiastes declares that "there is not a righteous man on earth who does what is right and never sins" (Eccl. 7:20). Isaiah explains that "all our righteous acts are like filthy rags" (Isa. 64:6).

3. **Righteousness is what God requires of us.** His standard is absolute. That is the thrust of Paul's argument in the first three chapters of Romans. He shows that Gentiles are accountable to God because they have chosen to suppress the light they have received through nature and conscience. Jews cannot feel superior because they have the Law. That, of course, is a great privilege (Rom. 3: 1-2), but it only serves to compound their guilt (Rom. 2:12-13). Listen to the way Paul summarizes:

We have already made the charge that Jews and Gentiles alike are under sin. Now we know that whatever the law says, it says to those who are under the law, so that every mouth may be silenced and the whole world may be held accountable to God. Therefore no-one will be declared righteous in his sight by observing the law; rather, through the law we become conscious of sin (Rom. 3: 9, 19-20).

4. **Righteousness is what God himself provides for us.** This is the whole point of Paul's argument in Romans. He builds step by step and them makes his key declaration, "But now a righteousness from God, apart from law, has been made known, to which the Law and the Prophets testify. This righteousness from God comes through faith in Jesus Christ to all who believe" (Rom. 3:21-22).

Paul remembers the time when he made a futile attempt to establish his own credentials before God. He could declare that he was faultless in regard to "legalistic righteousness." But he discovered to his joy "a righteousness which is through faith in Christ—a righteousness that comes from God and is by faith" (Phil. 3:6, 9). Later he mourned that his unbelieving compatriots had missed the point altogether: "Since they did not know the righteousness that comes from God and sought to establish their own, they did not submit to God's righteousness. Christ is the end of the law so that there may be righteousness for everyone who believes" (Rom 10:3- 4).

The Basis of this Righteousness
Paul explains the basis of this righteousness: "God made him who had no sin to be sin for us, so that in him we might become the righteousness of God" (2 Cor. 5:21). Here is what was happening on the cross. God looked upon his Son and said, "The wages of sin is death. You must die!" so he could look at you and me and say, "The gift of God is eternal life. You may live!"

Each of these titles of God emphasizes an important truth about God's nature. But this one probably tells us more of what we really *need* to know that any of the others, because it places the accent on what God has done for us in Christ. It conveys the lengths to which God has gone to procure your salvation and mine. He is *Yahweh Tsidqenu*--the LORD Our Righteousness. He is himself completely righteous, but the designation given to the Branch, the Son of David, is "The LORD *our* Righteousness." For that to be possible there had to be an incarnation, a perfect human life, and a substitutionary death. When we say, "*Yahweh Tsidqenu*" we are, in fact, declaring the gospel in just two words.

In A Nutshell

Summary

Isaiah, Jeremiah, and Zechariah all spoke about one who was to come and calls him the Branch. Isaiah associates him with righteousness (Isa. 11:4-5). Jeremiah describes him as "a righteous Branch" and says, "This is the name by which he will be called, 'Yahweh Tsidqenu—The LORD our Righteousness'" (Jer. 23:6). Zechariah was instructed to enact a sign—constructing a crown for the high priest, who was described as the Branch and declared to be "symbolic of things to come" (Zech. 3:8; 6:12).

As God's progressive revelation unfolds, we see that Jesus is indeed *Yahweh Tsidqenu*. His righteousness is imputed to us. Because of him God sees us and treats us as if we were as righteous as Jesus himself (2 Cor. 5:21; 1 Pet. 3:18).

A Prayer

LORD, you are righteous in all your ways. Your righteousness is everlasting. We acknowledge that we have no righteousness of our own. But you have gone to such great lengths to impute your righteousness to us. You are just. You could not simply declare us righteous. But you demonstrated your justice by presenting Jesus as a sacrifice of atonement on our behalf.

I know that it was because of your mercy that you saved us and not because of righteous things that we have done (Titus 3:5). Thank you that I can be clothed in the righteousness that comes from you and is by faith (Phil. 3:9).

As one who has been saved by grace through faith, I pray that the righteousness of Jesus will be evident in my life. I rejoice that I am now your "workmanship created in Christ Jesus to do good works" (Eph 2:10). Lord you are *our* righteousness. We give you the honour that is due your name.

Amen.

יְהוָה מְקַדִּשְׁכֶם
Yahweh Meqaddishchem
15

The LORD Who Sanctifies You

Just what does the word holiness mean to you? What does Scripture mean when it says, "Without holiness, no one will see the Lord" (Heb. 12:14; Matt. 5:8)? The word "holiness" (or "sanctification") has negative connotations for many of us. Kenneth Prior remarked, pertinently:

For many people, the word, if it conveys anything at all, revives memories of stained-glass windows depicting pale and unhealthy-looking faces with bones clearly visible under a thin layer of flesh. . . . Always present, of course, is the inevitable halo to underline the utter impracticability of the whole idea.[1]

We need to retrieve the word from its unfortunate associations. The good news is: (1) holiness is a wonderful and winsome quality that doesn't make you any less human; in fact, one could argue that it makes you more human, and (2) holiness is not something you have to achieve in your own strength. It's not "our part of the bargain." God reveals himself as *Yahweh Meqaddishchem*—the LORD who sanctifies you (makes you holy). The truth contained in this name of God is both liberating and empowering.

Passage and References

Passages: **Exod. 19:1-6; 31:12-13**; Lev. 22:9; 15, 16, 31-33; **Rom. 6:11-14; 8:1-4.**

References
   Matt. 5:17-20, 21-48; **Rom. 12:1-2**; 1 Cor. 1:30-31; **2 Cor. 3:7-18**; Gal. 5:22-23; Phil. 2:12-13; Col. 1:28-29; 1 Thess. 5:23-24; 1 Pet. 1:13- 16; **2 Pet. 1:3-11.**

Questions

1.   What is the first thing that comes into your mind when you hear the word "holiness" or "sanctification"?

2.   What do you think the Bible means when it says that God is holy?

3.   Do you think holiness or sanctification means more than "set apart"? If so, what does it mean?

4. God's children in the Old Testament were expected to be holy. So are we. But in what way, if any, are we at an advantage over them?

5. To your mind, what is the relationship between being born again (being indwelt by the Holy Spirit) and being sanctified?

6. Which of the following options do you think is most accurate?

Option 1: When we come to Jesus, God saves us, forgiving us and declaring us righteous. Having received mercy we are responsible to live lives that are pleasing to him. So, in response to his grace, we have to make every effort to live lives worthy of our high calling. It was up to him to save us. It is now up to us to live lives of obedience and holiness. We who celebrate his part realize that we have to do ours.

Option 2: The process of sanctification starts at the rebirth when the Holy Spirit takes up residence within us. Without his loving activity we can never be holy. But we need to cooperate with the Spirit ("walk in the Spirit"). There are some things we need to avoid like the plague. But, for the most part, we need to utilize the "means of grace" (everything that feeds our spiritual lives).

Option 3: "Sanctification" is what God does *in* us, just as much as justification was what God did *for* us. Any effort on our part will interfere with the process and put us back under the law. We have to surrender to God and trust him. He then works in us and we don't have to "strive" and fail. We may even have an experience of "entire sanctification" in which he takes over and we go from being defeated Christians to victorious Christians.

In your opinion, what is wrong with the other two options? More importantly, what makes your choice the best one?

7.   If it is true that (1) only the Lord can make us holy, and (2) we are not passive recipients of holiness but active participants in it, what sort of things can we do to co-operate with the Holy Spirit, working out the salvation he is working in us (Phil. 2:12-13)?

Comment

When Moses approached the burning bush he was told to remove his sandals because he was standing on holy ground (Exod. 3:5). From then on the word "holy" is used with frequency in Scripture. By examining its usage we are able to obtain a picture of what sanctification (holiness) is and how God himself enables us to be holy. We need to understand the concept before we consider how the Lord sanctifies us.

The Meaning of Holiness
As with any biblical concept that is used in different contexts, we
need to take account of the various strands of teaching concerning
holiness in order to obtain a comprehensive and balanced
understanding. A consistent picture emerges. For the sake of clarity
I shall make five comments about the term, in logical sequence.

1.   **Holiness is not some otherworldly quality that we acquire
through idealism and self-discipline.** In the opening paragraph I
referred to the caricature of holiness described by Kenneth Prior.
Fortunately Prior immediately gives us a healthier perspective:

The holy men of the Bible are miles removed from such popular
misconceptions. Instead of their being weak and anaemic, we find
they are often tough with sun-burnt faces, like Elijah, John the Baptist
and, be it reverently suggested, our Lord himself. . . . Holiness, when
rightly understood, is an attractive quality, not something forbidding
and inhuman. James Philip rightly observes: "The greatest saints of
God have been characterised, not by haloes and an atmosphere of
distant unapproachability (sic), but by their humanity. They have
been intensely human and lovable people with a twinkle in their
eyes."[2]

The association of holiness with self-imposed restrictions and
asceticism is unfortunate and unbiblical.

2.   **In its most basic sense, to be holy means to be set apart or
dedicated for a specific purpose.** An article may be dedicated for
special use and described as holy (Zech. 14:20-21). So may a place or
a day or an observance for that matter (Exod. 3:5; 15:13; 20:8;
30:31). People who are set aside or consecrated may also be
described as holy (Exod. 19:6; Num. 16:5; Luke 1:70). But, obviously,

the word means more than set-apartness. The contexts in which it is used indicate that there is an important moral component to holiness.

3.   **God himself is said to be holy**. He is frequently referred to as "the Holy One of Israel" (Psa. 89:18; Isa. 35:15). Holiness is one of God's attributes; some believe it is his primary attribute. When Isaiah saw the Lord, he heard the seraphim calling out, "Holy, holy, holy. . . ." (Isa. 6:1-7). Isaiah never forgot that vision. For him God is "the Holy One of Israel" (Isa. 30:11, 12, 15; 40:25; 43:3, 14-15; 57:15). As sinful creatures, we cannot but conceive of God as "different" from us, set apart in the sense of his otherness. Some of the theologians of the 20th century rightly stressed the fact that God is "wholly other." It is clumsy terminology, but part of God's transcendence, his exaltation above his creation, is his perfect holiness.

4.   **Holiness, as an attribute of God, is indescribably glorious**. From a negative point of view, it is the absence of impurity or corruption. From a positive point of view it connotes magnificent purity and splendour. The Psalmist encourages us to "worship the LORD in the beauty (splendour) of holiness" (Psa. 96:9). When we are given a picture of the throne of God, we see resplendent heavenly beings worshipping him. "Day and night they never stop saying, 'Holy, holy, holy is the Lord Almighty, who was, and is, and is to come'" (Rev. 4:8).

5.   **Holiness in God's children is an attractive quality.** It is not merely a sterile and dull absence of sin but the vibrant and glorious presence of goodness. There can be no element of self-righteousness (which is ugly) in true holiness. In the final analysis, to be holy is to be like Jesus, to be *Christlike.*

The Process of Holiness

In the Old Testament God made it clear that his people needed to be holy in order to be in fellowship with him (Exod. 19:6; Lev. 20:7, 26). But he also made it abundantly clear that he himself would make them holy (Lev. 22:32). Some believe that God set the bar very high in the Old Testament but gave his people little or no help to actually achieve the high standard. That's not completely accurate. His provision of a homeland, his law and the institutions of Israel were all there to help Israel live as his holy people (Exod. 19:6; Deut. 28:1-14).

They failed, not because God had failed to provide them with the means, but because our condition is such that all the external help in the world is not enough. Something more is needed if we are to live lives of commitment and obedience. Both the need and the provision of that need are described, especially by Jeremiah and Ezekiel (Jer. 31:31-34; Ezek. 36:25-27). We need to be changed *from the inside.*

When we turn to the New Testament, we notice that Jesus in no way lowered the standard (Matt. 5:17-20). He emphasized single-minded devotion to God (Matt 6:24). The same theme is present throughout the New Testament. Yes, God's grace is emphasized but this raises the bar even higher (Rom. 12:1-2; Eph. 2:8-10; 4:1-6, 17; Jam. 2:14- 26; 1 John 3:1-10).

The essential difference is spelled out in unambiguous terms. In 2 Corinthians 3, Paul contrasts the Old and New Covenant regimes. Under the Old Covenant, the "letter" was front and centre. Under the New, the role of the Holy Spirit is crucial. The "letter" (i.e. the law) kills, not because it is defective but because we cannot keep it

(Rom. 7:7-12; 2 Cor. 3:6; Gal. 3:10-14, 21-22). The subject is discussed in considerable detail in Romans 6, 7, and 8. In chapter 6, Paul makes it clear that "sin shall not be [our] master" because we are "alive to God in Christ Jesus" (Rom. 6:11-14). But in chapter 7, he provides us with an all-too-familiar picture of defeat when we endeavour to live righteous lives by keeping the law in our own strength.

In chapter 8, he describes life through the Holy Spirit: "What the law was powerless to do in that it was weakened by the sinful nature, God did by sending his own Son in the likeness of sinful humanity to be a sin offering" (Rom. 8:3). The passage teaches us that Jesus bore our sin and guilt thereby satisfying the demands of the law. But it also indicates that the practical outworking of this is that we "do not live according to the sinful nature but according to the Spirit" (Rom. 8:4). As we read on in the chapter, it is clear that the work of God's Spirit within us is the key to a life of sanctification.

The All-Important Truth
Too often, one all-important truth is overlooked. *It is just as impossible for us to live holy lives, lives pleasing to God, as it was for us to be declared righteous by keeping the law.* But, from the outset, God has declared himself to be the one who makes it possible for us to be holy. He who says, "Be holy, keep my commandments," also says, "I am *Yahweh Mekaddishchem* (I am the LORD who makes you holy)."

It's a little like my old camera. Before the advent of digital technology, cameras worked on a simple principle. Inside the camera was a small chamber in which there was no light whatsoever. You inserted a roll of light-sensitive film which was stretched across the back of the dark chamber. When you took a photograph, you heard a clicking sound; it was the sound of a mechanism that opened the shutter for a fraction of a second allowing light to pass into the camera though the lens. The light took the form of an image and, in a moment, the image made an impression on the film. You had "captured" the scene. But you did not yet have a picture. The film was later removed and developed in a dark-room. It was exposed to light and chemicals under controlled conditions. Slowly but surely the image began to appear. If you had been able to watch this development in the dark-room, you would have seen the image sharpen until the picture was a clear representation of the image created in the film by the refracted light.

Jesus insisted that we must be born again for a very good reason. The rebirth involves a change of heart, a change wrought in us by God himself. It's as though the light comes into our lives and makes an indelible impression. *Regeneration* or being born again has been described as the "act of God whereby the governing disposition of the soul is made holy."[3] But that is only the beginning of the process. By exposure to the right conditions the image is developed. *Sanctification* further develops the image instilled in the flash of regeneration. It has been defined as the "continuous process whereby the holy disposition imparted in regeneration is maintained and strengthened."[4] Through the ongoing work of the Holy Spirit, God transforms us into the likeness of his Son (Rom. 8:28-30; 2 Cor. 3:18).

What is absolutely essential to the process is the activity of the Holy Spirit within us. There is no neat formula, no magical moment, which places us in the "entirely sanctified" category. From the time we are born again, we are viewed as "saints" (sanctified ones). That's because the holiness of Jesus has been imputed to us and we have been cleansed (Heb. 10:14; 1 Cor. 6:11). Some distinguish between "positional" and "experiential" sanctification; that's fine, so long as we realize that Scripture doesn't allow us the luxury of speaking about positional sanctification unless the process of experiential sanctification is underway.

Sanctification is the work of the Spirit in us, but we are not simply passive recipients of God's sanctifying activity, being worked 'on' rather than 'in.' We can and should do certain things to advance the process. It really does not help to try to distinguish between the part God plays in our sanctification and the part we play. Scripture does not allow for such a distinction and if we try to invent one, we shall probably take ourselves back into legalistic bondage. God's work and our cooperative response are so closely related as to be, to all intents and purposes, indistinguishable. Paul's prayer for the Thessalonians is that "God himself, the God of peace, will sanctify you through and through and that your whole spirit, soul and body will be kept blameless at the coming of our Lord Jesus Christ." He immediately adds, "The one who calls you is faithful and he will do it" (1 Thess. 5:23-24). But that great benediction is preceded by a list of practical instructions, the last of which is, "Avoid every kind of evil." He urges the Philippians: "Continue to work out your salvation with fear and trembling for it is God who works in you to will and to act according to his good pleasure" (Phil. 2:12-13). Perhaps the clearest expression of the cooperative nature of the process is found in Paul's statement to the Colossians, "To this end *I labor*, struggling with all *his* energy, which so powerfully works in me" (Col. 1:29; emphasis added).

A Positive Approach
From a practical point of view, a positive approach achieves far more than a negative one. There are certain things we know we should not do. It is within our power to avoid them and we should certainly do

so. We know they will not help us in our walk with the Lord. But if this is all we do (or don't do) the emphasis is negative and we may become legalistic and joyless or even self-righteous. Simply avoiding certain practices does not constitute sanctification. What's more, if we try in our own strength to "battle our giants" or to overcome deep-seated habits or attitudes, this often leads to the kind of defeat described in Romans 7:14-24. That is why Paul lays such emphasis on "living by the Spirit" (Gal. 5:16). He describes what the Holy Spirit does in us: "The fruit of the Spirit is love, joy peace, patience, kindness, goodness, faithfulness, gentleness, and self-control." Most significantly he adds, "Against such things there is no law" (Gal. 5:22- 23). If the focus is on the Spirit's control, and not the letter of the law, we fulfill the spirit of the law. The emphasis is on what we are, rather than what we do!

It's not that the commandments fall away. James, for example, makes it clear that there is a "royal law found in Scripture" (Jam. 2:8), and John tells us that if we say we know the Lord and don't keep his commandments, we are liars (1 John 2:4). Paul instructs us to "avoid every kind of evil" (1 Thess. 5:22). It's a question of *how* this is achieved. Think of some of the Ten Commandments: "Do not murder," "Do not steal," "Do not bear false testimony," and "Do not covet. . . ." (Exod. 20:13-17). "The fruit of the Spirit is love. . . ." That means that as the Holy Spirit influences me from within, the fruit of love grows in my life. How can I steal from one whom I love and how can I covet their possessions?

As simple as it may sound, we grow most not by intentionally avoiding sin but by exposing ourselves to God's activity through various "means of grace." Everything that will build us up, feed us spiritually, influence our thinking, and transform our attitudes will help the process of growth. Some of the negatives will drop out of our lives without our even realizing it. We will change as the process of transformation continues. No haloes will appear around our heads but the beauty of Jesus will be seen in us. Put simply, if we do what we *can* do, God will do what we *can't* do. Or better, he will enable us to do what we can't do.

This wonderful teaching, which is developed in the New Testament, is present in the Old. It is such an integral part of God's nature as *Yahweh*, our covenant LORD, that he even incorporates his sanctifying activity into his name: "Consecrate yourselves and be holy, because I am the LORD, your God. Keep my decrees and follow them. . . . I am *Yahweh Mekaddishchem*--the LORD who sanctifies you" (Exod. 31:13).

In A Nutshell

Summary
"Holiness" is a glorious attribute of God and it is what God requires of us. In the first place it is separation *from* what is ordinary of corrupt and separation *to* God himself. He sets us apart for his own use. But there is more to sanctification than "set-apart-ness." It is an attractive quality in which we become increasingly like the Lord. We cannot achieve this by emulation (our own effort). Sanctification entails God's work in us. It is the progressive transformation of our lives from within through the activity of the Holy Spirit. We are not passive instruments being worked "on" but active participants in the process, being worked "in."

God has always been *"Yahweh Mekaddishchem*—the LORD who sanctifies you." But his sanctifying work is especially evident under the New Covenant. The indwelling Spirit within us transforms us: "We, who with unveiled faces all reflect the Lord's glory, are being transformed into his likeness with ever-increasing glory, which comes from the Lord, who is the Spirit" (2 Cor. 3:18).

A Prayer

Father, we long for the beauty of Jesus to be seen in us. We are so grateful that you have given us your Spirit as a deposit guaranteeing our inheritance. We thank you that he not only testifies with our spirits that we are your children but also draws us closer to you and transforms us into your likeness.

I confess my need of you and present my body as a living sacrifice, holy and acceptable to you. I know that I am constantly bombarded by inducements to conform to the present evil age. But I want to be transformed by the renewing of my mind. Lord, like Paul, I know that "I have not already been made perfect, but I press on to take hold of that for which Christ Jesus took hold of me" (Phil. 3:12).

Let the beauty of Jesus be seen in me,
all his wondrous passion and purity.
O Thou Spirit divine,
all my nature refine,
till the beauty of Jesus
is seen in me.

Amen.

NOTES

[1] Kenneth Prior, *The Way of Holiness* (London: Inter-Varsity Press, 1967), 7.

[2] Ibid.

[3] A. H. Strong, *Systematic Theology* (Valley Forge: Judson, 1907), 809.

[4] Ibid., 869.

יְהוָה שָׁמָּה

Yahweh Shammah

16

The LORD is There

Yahweh Shammah—"the LORD is there" is actually a name given to the future city of God, but it conveys a very important truth about God himself. The city is special because of its name and its name is meaningful because it communicates to us the reality of God's presence. There can hardly be a more fitting way to conclude this study of the names of God than with a consideration of God as the one who is eternally present with his people.

Passage and References

Passage   Ezek. 43:1-7, 48:35.

References
   Gen. 28:10-19; Exod. 25:22; 40:34-35; 1 Kings 8:27;
2 Chron. 7:1- 3; John 4:21-24; 1 Cor. 3:16; 2 Cor. 6:16; **Eph. 2:19-22**;
Rev. 21:3, 22-23; 22:3-5.

Questions

1.   When you think of the temple (and the tabernacle before it) what is the first thing that comes to mind? And what else?

2. Ezekiel had the unenviable task of disabusing his compatriots who believed that Solomon's temple could never fall since God dwelt there. The temple did fall but God showed that his glory had departed *before* Nebuchadnezzar's forces leveled the place (Ezek 10:1-22; 11:22). At the end of the Book of Ezekiel, there is a detailed description of the temple and the glory of the LORD returns (Ezek 43:1-7). What does this tell us about, (1) God, and (2) the temple?

3. From Solomon's prayer at the dedication of the temple (1 Kings 8:10-13, 27-30), what do you think he believed about God's presence in the temple?

4. You may recall that one of the false charges brought against Jesus was that he spoke against the temple (Mark 14:5-59). Did he? (Mark 11:12-18; John 2:12-25)

5. Stephen was accused of speaking against Moses and the temple (Acts 6:12-14). What did Stephen actually say about the temple? (Acts 7:48-50; Isa 66:1-2)

6.   Do you think that a temple will be rebuilt in Jerusalem at some point in the future? Why/Why not? (Please don't get side-tracked on this one in the group and agree to differ if needs be, but do share your honest thoughts and questions).

7.   Do you think the messages of Ezekiel and Revelation (a giant temple; no temple) are compatible? If you say "Yes", how do you explain this difference of emphasis?

8.   What do you think Jesus meant when he spoke to the Samaritan woman at the well, and seemed to disparage the temple (John 4:21- 24)?

9.   Does a temple exist in the present (Eph 2:19-22)? Think of some implications for the church of this reality (1 Cor 3:16-17; 6:18-20; Eph 1:22-23).

10. When we gather to worship as a church, should we expect to become aware of the fact that we are standing on holy ground? What might this look like in practice?

Comment

Undoubtedly, God is omnipresent. The Psalmist celebrates this reality but he has more in mind than a metaphysical statement:

> Where can I go from your Spirit?
> Where can I flee from your presence?
> If I go to the heavens, you are there;
> if I make my bed in the depths, you are there.
> If I rise on the wings of the dawn,
> if I settle on the far side of the sea,
> even there your hand will guide me,
> your right hand will hold me fast.
> If I say, "Surely the darkness will hide me
> and the light become night around me,"
> even the darkness will not be dark to you;
> the night will shine like the day,
> for darkness is as light to you   (Ps. 139:7-12).

More than Omnipresence

God is everywhere but it is also true that he chooses to manifest his presence at particular times and places. Young Jacob left home for the first time and set out for the land of Haran. Imagine his churned-up emotions as he left his parental home at Beersheba. He travelled a day's journey, stopped for the night and fell asleep with a stone for his pillow. In a dream, he saw a stairway that reached from earth to heaven. Angels were ascending and descending on this stairway. Above it stood the LORD himself who reassured him regarding his protection and his promise.

When Jacob awoke from his sleep, he thought, "Surely the LORD is in this place, and I was not aware of it." He was afraid and said, "How awesome is this place! This is none other than the house of God; this is the gate of heaven." He called the place Bethel—"House of God" (Gen 28:16-17, 19). Clearly more is in view than God's omnipresence.

God gave very specific instructions regarding the construction of the tabernacle that formed the focal point of the worship of Israel as the tribes wandered in the Sinai Desert. It was to be erected right in the centre of the encampment of Israel. It consisted of an outer courtyard or enclosure and a sanctuary comprising a holy place and a most holy place. There, in the heart of the sanctuary, at the centre of the whole structure, in the Most Holy Place, the Ark of the Covenant was to be placed. The ark was a wooden chest containing the tablets of the law, a pot of manna and Aaron's rod. It was overlaid with gold. On top of it was an atonement cover made of pure gold on which there were two golden statuettes of cherubim facing inwards. The LORD said: "There, above the cover between the two cherubim that are over the ark of the Testimony, I will meet with you and give you all my commands for the Israelites" (Exod. 25:22).

When the tabernacle was completed, "the cloud covered the Tent of Meeting, and the glory of the LORD filled the tabernacle. Moses could not enter the Tent of Meeting because the cloud had settled upon it, and the glory of the LORD filled the tabernacle" (Exod. 40:34- 35). The same was true of the temple. In his prayer

King Solomon marvelled that God would stoop to live among his people: "But will God really dwell on earth? The heavens, even the highest heaven, cannot contain you. How much less this temple I have built!" (I Kings 8:27). Listen to what happened:

When Solomon finished praying, fire came down from heaven and consumed the burnt offering and the sacrifices, and the glory of the LORD filled the temple. The priests could not enter the temple of the LORD because the glory of the LORD filled it. When all the Israelites saw the fire coming down and the glory of the LORD above the temple, they knelt on the pavement with their faces to the ground, and they worshipped and gave thanks to the LORD, saying, "He is good; his love endures forever" (2 Chron. 7:1-3).

What was it that Elijah experienced in the cave at Mount Horeb?

The LORD said, "Go out and stand on the mountain in the presence of the LORD, for the LORD is about to pass by." Then a great and powerful wind tore the mountains apart and shattered the rocks before the LORD, but the LORD was not in the wind. After the wind there was an earthquake, but the LORD was not in the earthquake. After the earthquake came a fire but the LORD was not in the fire. And after the fire came a gentle whisper (the sound of a gentle quietness). When Elijah heard it, he pulled his cloak over his face and went out and stood at the mouth of the cave (I Kings 19:11-13).

He knew the difference between a display of nature's force and the presence of the LORD.

So, this is the picture that emerges: *God is present everywhere, but at certain times he chooses to manifest his presence in special ways at particular places.*

Ezekiel's vision

The prophets looked forward to a time when God would be present with his people for ever. This theme is found, for example, in Isaiah and repeated by prophets like Jeremiah, Joel and Zechariah (Isa. 65: 17-25; Jer. 31:31-34; Joel 3:17; Zech. 2:5; 14:8-9). Nowhere is it clearer than in the Book of Ezekiel. Ezekiel had an extremely difficult task. He and some of his compatriots had been taken into exile in Babylonia some years before the destruction of Jerusalem in 587 BC. But his fellow exiles were quite convinced that they would soon be back in Israel. For one thing, the temple was still standing and they were certain that because it was God's house it was impregnable. After all, his glory dwelt there. Some false prophets were assuring them that their exile would be of short duration. Ezekiel had to disabuse them. God gave him special visions which formed the basis of his message. The vision in chapter 10 is particularly significant:

The glory of the LORD rose from above the cherubim and moved to the threshold of the temple. The cloud filled the temple and the court was full of the radiance of the glory of the LORD. Then the glory of the LORD departed from over the threshold of the temple and stopped above the cherubim. . . . They stopped at the entrance to the east gate of the LORD'S house, and the glory of the LORD of Israel was above them. The glory of the LORD went up from within the city and stopped above the mountain from the east of it. I told the exiles everything the LORD had shown me (Ezek. 10:4, 18; 11:23, 25).

Toward the end of the book, Ezekiel is given a picture of the restoration of the city and the temple. It is appropriate, in view of the centrality of the temple as the dwelling place of God, that the restoration of God's presence should be described in terms of a reconstructed temple, which is described in great detail. The temple in the vision is massive; its dimensions are large enough to accommodate thirteen cathedrals (Ezek. 40-42). Significantly, it does not have a Most Holy Place! There is an intentional link with the prophecy of chapter 10. Clearly, the picture we are given looks way beyond any intermediate fulfilment to a more distant future.

I saw the glory of the God of Israel coming from the east. His voice was like the roar of rushing waters, and the land was radiant with his glory. The vision I saw was like the vision I had seen when he came to destroy the city . . . and I fell face down. The glory of the LORD entered the temple through the gate facing east. Then the Spirit lifted me up and brought me into the inner court and the glory of the LORD filled the temple. I heard someone speaking to me from inside the temple. He said, "Son of man, this is the place of my throne and the place for the soles of my feet. This is where I will live among the Israelites forever" (Ezek. 43:2-7).

And the name of the city from that time on will be: *Yahweh Shammah*--THE LORD IS THERE (Ezek. 48:35).

The Revelation
We hear the same message in Revelation, only in a different way. In view of the circumstances it was appropriate for Ezekiel to describe the future in terms of a huge city with a great temple. Living water flowed from under the threshold of the temple not only supporting vegetation but even giving life to the Dead Sea (Ezek. 47:1-12).

In the Apocalypse the same truth is conveyed in a way more appropriate to the subsequent revelation God has given us:

And I heard a loud voice from the throne saying, "Now the dwelling of God is with men, and he will live with them. They will be his people, and God himself will be with them and be their God." I did not see a temple in the city, because the Lord God Almighty and the Lamb are its temple. The city does not need the sun or moon to shine on it, for the glory of God gives it light and the Lamb is its lamp (Rev. 21:3, 22-23).

The throne of God and of the Lamb will be in the city, and his servants will serve him. They will see his face and his name will be on their foreheads. There will be no more night. . . . (Rev. 22:3-4).

There is an important point that stands out in all of this. God created mankind to enjoy fellowship with him. But that fellowship was disrupted by sin. He did not abandon us but we could not continuously live in his holy presence. He would meet with us at particular times and places, but there would be a limitation. Then, in the fullness of time, he came and lived among us as Emmanuel ("God with us"). John says he pitched his tent among us, using imagery that reminds us of the tabernacle (John 1:14).

In the remainder of this study we shall focus on the present, but first we need to note that at the end of history, all barriers are removed. *God dwells with his people permanently.* In the words of Ezekiel: "*Yahweh Shammah*—the LORD is there." In the words of the Apocalypse, "God's dwelling place is now among the people, and he will dwell with them. They will be his people, and God himself will be with them and be their God. . . . I did not see a temple in the city because the Lord God Almighty and the Lamb are its temple" (Rev. 21:3, 22). Well might we look forward to that great day!

God's Presence Today
In one way, we don't have to wait for that day. There is a place where God manifests his presence today. George Eldon Ladd has

written a book entitled, *The Presence of the Future.*[1] In it he shows that in a very real sense the future kingdom is present now. One day we will, so to speak, live in a city called *Yahweh Shammah.* In the New Jerusalem there will be no temple, no physical structure, as such. Important as it was, the temple was a temporary measure.

But, right here and now, God loves to meet with us. The New Testament teaches that we are the temple of the Holy Spirit. That's what Paul says to the Corinthians: "Don't you know that you yourselves are God's temple and that God's Spirit lives in you?" (I Cor. 3: 16) *We* are the temple of the living God. As God has said, "I will live in them and walk among them, and I will be their God, and they will be my people" (2 Cor. 6:16). Paul is even more explicit when he writes to the Ephesians: "In him the whole building rises to become a holy temple in the Lord. And in him you too are being built together to become a dwelling in which God lives by his Spirit" (Eph. 2:21-22).

Since the Day of Pentecost, we are able to experience the Lord's presence in a wonderful and very real way. The experience of his presence should not be a rare exception. *We* are his temple. He wants to manifest his glory among us. Yes, even now, we are conscious of limitations, limitations that will be completely removed in the New Jerusalem (Rom. 8:23-27; 2 Cor. 4:16-5:5). When we come to him in sincere worship, he makes his presence felt. It will not always be the same. He is, after all, God. We meet with him as a living person. We do not press a button or invoke a formula. We may expect to experience his presence in different ways according to our needs and his purpose in our lives. But, in one way and another, we can know that we are in his presence.

Whenever we meet in Jesus name, he is here, not just in the sense that he is omnipresent. We do not come just to reflect on his truth, or even to commemorate his deeds. We come to meet with him. And, strange as it may seem to us, the LORD really wants to meet with us. What an inestimable privilege to be in a place that can be described as *Yahweh Shammah*.

In A Nutshell

Summary
God, who is omnipresent, has chosen to manifest his presence in special ways and in particular places. Jacob became so aware of God's presence that he called the place where God met with him *Beth-El* (house of God). God's presence was manifested at the burning bush, in the tabernacle and the temple, and to people like Elijah. Jesus was to be called Emmanuel (God with us). He pitched his tent among us; "in Christ all the fullness of the Deity lives in bodily form" (John 1:14; Col. 2:9). God is now present with us by his Spirit (2 Cor. 6:16; Eph 2:20-22). But when his great plan of salvation reaches completion, and the estrangement we have experienced since our expulsion from Eden is over forever, God's dwelling is with us permanently (Rev. 21:1-4). Of that majestic city it will be said, "*Yahweh Shammah*—the LORD is there."

Right now we can experience his presence. This is especially true
when we meet together (Matt. 18:20; 1 Cor. 3:16-17;
Eph. 2:21- 22).

A Prayer

How lovely is your dwelling place,
LORD Almighty!
My soul yearns, even faints,
for the courts of the LORD;
my heart and my flesh cry out
for the living God.

Better is one day in your courts
than a thousand elsewhere;
I would rather be a doorkeeper in the house of my God
than dwell in the tents of the wicked (Psa. 84:1, 2, 10).

Lord, it never ceases to amaze us that you choose to dwell with your
people. We look forward to the day when the limitations of the
present are a thing of the past and your dwelling place is
permanently among your people (Rev. 21:3). But even now we thank
you that we are being built together to become a dwelling in which
you live by your Spirit" (Eph. 2:22). Lord, please help us to become
more and more aware of your presence among us.

Amen.

NOTES

[1] George Eldon Ladd, *The Presence of the Future*, rev. ed. (Grand Rapids, MI: William B. Eerdmans, 1996).

www.ingramcontent.com/pod-product-compliance
Lightning Source LLC
Chambersburg PA
CBHW071959040426
42447CB00009B/1409